Longest Hours
thoughts while waiting

a Silver Boomer Book

collection compiled by:

Melody Mann
Judy Callarman
Becky Haigler
Barbara B. Rollins

www.SilverBoomerBooks.com
~§~
SilverBoomerBooks@gmail.com

Library of Congress Control Number: 2013944191
ISBN: 978-1-937905-18-7

Printed in the United States of America

Table of Contents

"'For a while' is a phrase whose length can't be measured. At least by

that the years teach us patience – that the shorter our time, the greater

requires the willingness to bear uncertainty, to carry within oneself the unanswered question, lifting the heart to God about it whenever it in-

Hearts' Vigil

Judy Callarman

Our third child, Mark, was born about seven p.m. on January 7, 1975. When the doctor first showed him to me, I could see how beautiful and perfect he was. The only thing that worried me was that he was purplish blue all over, but he cried and breathed and moved. Nobody gave any indication that anything might be wrong with him.

The next morning, I waited impatiently for a nurse to bring him to my room. No one came. I pushed my call button and asked why. The nurse was vague, saying, "Oh, the doctor is checking him. He'll be out soon."

Two years earlier when I had taken Mark's big brother Brian to the pediatrician for his well check at the age of four weeks, Dr. Schaefer listened hard to his heart. He announced that my baby boy had a "serious" heart murmur – a slight heart defect – that would need extensive checking and probably, eventually, heart surgery, but for now was not a problem. I cried. We worried a little during my pregnancy with Mark, but doctors assured us it would be quite unlikely that Mark would also have a heart defect.

About 10:30 the morning after Mark's birth, Dr. Schaefer came into my room – no baby yet. He sat down and sighed, rubbing his freckled forehead. "I'd

my lips, / It will surely never die / As I'm waiting here for you / until

rather kick myself all the way around the block than to have to tell you this," he said. I knew, and the tears began to flow. "Your baby has a very serious heart defect that causes him to be blue. You'll need to take him to Children's Medical Center next week for a heart cath to see what it is."

When Mark was only nine days old and weighed six pounds, we took him to Dallas for a heart catheterization, a test to determine the extent of his problems. The test showed that he had a complicated heart defect known as Tetralogy of Fallot. That meant four things were wrong, resulting in low oxygen levels in his blood. A hole between the two bottom chambers of his heart was about the size of a quarter. Since it was so large, the blood flowed the wrong direction through the hole and to his body, instead of to his lungs, causing his body to receive blood with too little oxygen. I loved him with a fierce love and had the feeling that if I sat and held him tightly, rocking and singing, he would be all right.

Doctors told us Mark would need open-heart surgery when he was "big enough." In 1975, the instruments available for the surgery were too large for tiny babies. After all, only 23 years had passed since the heart-lung machine made possible the first successful operation to repair a congenital heart defect in 1952. They said we would wait until Mark grew as big as possible before his total repair, "keeping tabs on him all along."

Our lives took on a different hue as we tried to maintain a normal life, knowing we could lose Mark. Now even though the waiting was like torture, we knew we had to do it. There was no use in ranting or stomping about – although I cried many tears.

Until then, we had managed not to think much about Brian's heart because he had always been big, healthy, and rugged. After his first checkup, we knew that Brian too would eventually have surgery. His defect was simply a small slit-shaped hole between the two bottom chambers – a ventricular septal defect. Doctors assured us that after their repair surgery, both boys should be fine, although they would do well always to remember that "cars with overhauled engines can't run the Indian-apolis 500."

We waited almost with held breath to see if Mark would be able to breastfeed. He could, much to my joy. But after only three months, he declared an end to it at 5:30 one morning because it was hard work and his nose was stuffy. I searched for an easy-flow kind of nipple to be sure he could suck the formula easily. Finally I found one with three holes, and he thrived, although he was small. He often developed respiratory ailments with coughing, congestion, and fever because, as Dr. Schaefer explained, his lungs stayed a bit saturated. He had occasional "tet" or "blue" spells when he struggled to catch his breath and passed out briefly.

We waited to see if we could keep his heart beating steadily and hard enough to avoid the fainting spells by giving him Inderol, a derivative of digitalis. Every month we took him to the local hospital lab to check his hemo-globin level, because his low blood-oxygen level caused his red blood cells to increase and his blood to thicken. If it became too thick, his heart would not be able to pump it.

When Mark was eight months old, the doctors decided we could not wait any longer, so we headed to Dallas. Because he was still too small for the total

repair, he had a Blalock-Tausig shunt, a terrible tempo-
rary procedure in which a branch of the artery to the
right arm was disconnected and attached to the pulmo-
nary artery to increase oxygenated blood flow to his
body. Immediately, we could see something was wrong.
A small, strange rattle came at the end of each breath,
and his big brown eyes looked alarmed.

We waited all day while technicians tested his blood
gases hourly and doctors stood around him and
puzzled. By the next morning, my baby's eyes were
constantly open and unfocused, and his breaths were
far between and shallow. He was dying right before our
eyes. I wanted to scream. They announced that the
arterial connection they had made was too big, causing
his lungs to fill with fluid. They would now go back in
and cut it down by half.

That was successful, but he was still a little blue. For
three weeks, we waited while he was in ICU, sedated,
on a respirator, letting his lungs dry out. We stayed with
him as often as we could, but we could visit only every
two hours during the day. I am a constant reader, but I
could not read there in the waiting room. I knitted and
talked to other distraught parents. We decided it was
like being in a long shipwreck together. Finally we got to
take him home, our miracle baby.

When Mark was three in 1978, his hemoglobin level
was again high, so it was time for his total repair. We
could not bring ourselves to take him back to Dallas, so
we took him to the Texas Children's Hospital in Houston
where the internationally known surgeon Dr. Denton
Cooley did the work.

Mark came through the surgery well without too
many complications. I suffered from anxiety-induced

was going to do, and what I was going to be. I was standing there,

stomach cramps and diarrhea during his four-week stay, waiting for his heart to learn to beat properly. He was finally nice and pink although he was weak and occasionally pale for a few weeks. He gradually became a rough-and-tumble boy like his brother.

The next fall, six-year-old Brian had his repair, also in Houston. After only a week, Brian was bouncing up and down the hall and racing other children in wheelchairs.

In all those hospital waiting rooms, we met parents whose children had incurable cancers, deadly blood diseases, and impossible brain abnormalities. We learned to be very grateful for relatively simple heart defects that could be repaired. I began to understand how people can comfort each other by simply caring and listening.

Life has been easier and more normal in most ways since then. Growing up, both boys played hard, gave their big sister Leigh a hard time, and were active in organized sports. Now Brian is 40 and Mark is 38. Between them, they have seven children, none of whom have heart defects. They and their families all work hard at keeping themselves in good shape physically with lots of jogging, skiing, and hiking. Their overhauled engines work well, although they make strange pumping sounds through stethoscopes and Mark has no pulse in his right arm because of the shunt.

When our children were in college, they and I became Christians, and I realized God's power and grace kept us safe during those early years and enabled us to bear the aching in our hearts. During all that waiting and despairing and hoping and loving, something happened to my heart, although I was not

waiting for someone to do something, till I realized the person I was

fully aware of it then. My heart grew into a new shape and size – out of all its bounds. It took into itself new meaning, and flowing love from the Source of all love rose there like a tidal river and encircled my children. The strength of love held us up during our hearts' vigil.

Minutes into a Three-Hour Journey
Jennifer Clark

Are we there yet?
our son asks as
the car window frames

row upon row of
cornstalks the color of sand.
Like bitter fingers

they poke through
hardened earth
bent and hollow now,

having given up months ago
plump, baby kernels
nestled in fine silk.

Are we there yet?

Still, rows flicker by.
Snow like spilled diamonds
glitters amongst the broken

husks of hands that
hold nothing but time, barely
rustling the same story.

Are we there yet?

Perhaps we are.
Let us stop
for a moment,

jump over barbed-wire fencing
and run with abandon.
Let us say we are here.

Fear

Cathy Baker

A coiled predator,
fear constricts
my reality.
Relentless "what if's?"
course like venom
through my veins.
I tire of the taste
of lingering excuses.
Will I ever receive unraveling relief?

Waving at Trains

Rosie Garland

On the bridge, I wave at every woman.
Half the population of Great Britain;
thirty million according to Miss Grant.
A hundred women in each train,
two trains on the way

to school, three on the walk home,
makes five hundred; times five days a week
equals two thousand five hundred
which goes into thirty million
too many times for me to work out.

I scratch the numbers in my notebook,
stringing beads of zeros across the bottom
of each page to calculate how long
I've got to do this before I've waved
to every single one.

Then I'll know that one of them was her.
The woman who gave birth to me
three thousand seven hundred and twelve days ago
(including leap years), then gave me away.
She will see something familiar
in the way I flag my hand, and know.

~§~ *"The whole time you thought you were waiting on God, but the*

Waiting for Validation

Wendy Estelle-Bialek

I can't believe I'm sitting here in the bushes waiting for proof that will convince me and my shrink that I'm not crazy. Waiting like this brings me back to when I first met Richard. I was seventeen years old and more immature teen than responsible young woman – a neophyte in matters of love and war. I was just a kid with a good bit of spunk; but unfortunately, not much common sense when it came to the allure and charisma of my high school's football coach.

He came to the school in the middle of my senior year when I was on top of the food chain in the dog-eat-dog world of teenage academia. I had the looks and the grades, and the attitude that went along with them. It's hard to believe in less than two years I've turned into the kind of person who would hide, crouched in the bushes, waiting for some sort of validation of my own sanity. Yet here I sit – waiting.

Back then it all seemed like a fairytale. I was the pretty, pompom-shaking, cheerleader princess, capturing the heart of the unbearably sexy, play-book-wielding Prince Charming. People tried to tell me I was being silly and that Richard had no interest in me. I can still hear Ms. Stevens, my cheerleading coach, urging me to snap out of my fantasy.

"I've talked to him about you, Rachel. He thinks you're a good kid, maybe a little misguided, but a good kid – not a love interest," she said. "I know you're young and you don't see it; but trust me, if you go around telling people you're secretly seeing Coach Hanson things could get ugly – fast. You're a kid in high school for God's sake. Do you know what would happen to him if anyone thought he was seeing you?"

I remember sitting there while she droned on, feeling certain it was just her jealousy talking. After all, at nearly thirty years old she was already over the hill. She was so bitter I almost felt sorry for her. She did make a valid point about the perceived inappropriateness of our affair. Yes, he was a teacher involved with a student. It would have made a great Lifetime Television movie. But it didn't turn into a scandal – because I waited.

I listened to him when he insisted we wait to declare our love publicly. He denies it, but he would whisper so sweetly in my ear as we lay tangled in the sheets after making love.

"You just have to wait a little longer, Rache – then you can tell the world about us. You don't want me to get in trouble, do you? I'm way too pretty for prison," he would say. So – I waited.

I did tell a few friends I was having an affair with an older man. But just like Coach Stevens, they thought I was making it up. That's what seemed crazy to me. Why would I make it up? I was the princess. I could have any boy I wanted. I didn't need to imagine a lover. I decided to keep my mouth shut anyway. If Richard wanted me to wait, I would wait.

The obnoxious vibration of bass thumping from a car stereo startles me. I tuck myself farther back into the bushes until the car passes. It's colder than I thought it would be. I wish I had thought to grab a sweater, but that really wasn't an option. I check the time on the bank clock at the corner. It's 9:45 p.m. and there's still no sign of him. I'll wait a little longer.

Waiting back then was much more fun and more comfortable. Because our affair was taboo, the anticipation of seeing him was exhilarating. I didn't mind waiting for him to pick the perfect location for our secret rendezvous – usually right here – or waiting until it was dark so we wouldn't be seen. I really didn't even mind waiting for graduation if it meant I could be with him whenever I wanted.

I should have realized it was a joke when I finally graduated and he told me I still had to wait. In the beginning he had been so warm and compassionate when we talked about our future, basking in the afterglow of our lovemaking. But then when he was done with me, he turned into someone I didn't know.

timeless." R.S. Thomas ~§~ "Patience is learned through waiting."

If I saw him on the street or followed him home, he'd say I was stalking him. Sometimes he was kind, but other times he was mean and hurtful, saying that I was crazy and needed to be put away. How could he say such things? Didn't he remember the love we shared? Did he forget the way he undressed me that first time, kissing every inch of my body, telling me I would be his forever? Did I imagine it?

It was during one of his ugly outbursts that he had me arrested. As a birthday surprise I had let myself into his apartment while he was out and I waited for him. I wore a negligée made of angelic white lace and satin and my make-up was almost non-existent. I knew I had to look innocent for him or he wouldn't want me anymore. I sat there with a birthday cake on my lap, candles ready to be lit. I waited for three hours.

When I heard the front door open, I lit the candles – then I heard her voice. I thought I was hearing things. What was Coach Stevens doing here? The next thing I knew the two of them were stumbling into the bedroom, frantically undressing each other. They tumbled onto the bed before they noticed I was sitting there with my cake and candles.

Everyone says I'm the crazy one, but if you ask me, Richard is the one who's certifiable. He ranted and raved like a lunatic, practically foaming at the mouth as he screamed at me to get out of his house.

He acted as if his life depended on it, begging Coach Stevens to believe he had nothing to do with me being there. She believed him. I'm not sure why I didn't try to defend myself. I should have told her it wasn't the first time I had been in his bed, but I didn't. I just waited for the police to come and take me away.

The police took me to the hospital that night and the doctors made me stay. That was six months ago. They still won't let me leave, even though I've told them everything about Richard. The more I talk, the crazier they think I am. Oh, they don't say crazy. No, they say I'm delusional and live in a false state of reality. They didn't believe me about this place, either.

I can't stop shivering now and I feel like I should just give up. What am I waiting for anyway? I poke my head out to check the time again just as a police cruiser rounds the corner. He sees me, stops in front of my hiding spot and gets out.

"Miss, are you all right?" he asks.

"Yes, I'm fine," I say, staying in the bushes, not wanting to reveal myself.

"Can you step out here so I can make sure you're okay?"

If I've ever acted insanely it is now. I step out wearing nothing but a hospital gown and plastic slippers, but I act as though I am dressed appropriately.

forgotten. It wants to break open the ripe fruit when it has hardly fin-

"I'm fine, Officer. I was just leaving," I say and start to walk away.

In a matter of moments he has me cuffed and sitting in the backseat of the cruiser – waiting.

Someone has called in my suspicious activity. The hospital hadn't suggested the police look for me here. They still don't believe me.

We are waiting at the traffic light when I finally see Richard. He is turning onto the street we are leaving. I recognize the girl with him. It isn't Coach Stevens. It is Vicki Wilson. She was on the freshman squad my senior year, and that makes her about sixteen years old now. I'm sure she had been eagerly waiting for the signal to sneak out and meet him, while I was waiting for a sign to authenticate my life.

Richard and I make eye contact as the cars pass. I can tell in an instant he knows I wouldn't mention seeing him with her. He can see that my need for self-recovery is greater than my need to save her. But I can also see in his eyes that he knows a day will come when I'll be strong enough to fight. When that day will be is anyone's guess. But one thing is certain. He will be the one – waiting.

Waiting for Y2K

Christine Collier

It doesn't seem possible it's been thirteen years since Y2K. The years that followed had many gripping headlines, but none that seemed to go on as long as this subject matter did. It lasted a full year.

The ending of the Millennium in connection with computers was truly unknown territory. What would happen when the clocks changed and 1999 became 2000? We surely heard enough speculation. Would our power grids crash, the water systems go dry, banks fail, planes fall out of the sky, with people rioting in the streets because of dwindling food supplies? Late-night television host David Letterman warned us on December 31, 1999, that "stuff's gonna 'splode," in his hilarious top ten list concerning Y2K. Also, that the Big Dipper would fall from the sky and kill a guy in Sweden.

Since I kept a journal for many years, I wrote about the endless chatter concerning Y2K. My husband kept saying he didn't think anything would happen at midnight, but still, he must have been concerned. He bought tons of canned veggies and gallons of water. It took years to use them up.

ceived; the fruit that seemed so precious is still green on the inside, and

My excerpts from 1999 are listed below. I'm so glad I taped into my journal news articles and cartoons that complemented the entries. I would never have remembered how much fear was mixed with humor over this subject matter.

August 23, 1999 — We're in Niagara Falls, Canada, for our 30th wedding anniversary. We had a wonderful dinner overlooking a fantastic view of the Falls. The restaurant has a huge clock in the entrance. A sign above it counts down the hours and seconds to the Millennium. It's hard to take your eyes off it.

September 10, 1999 — Feared 9-9-99 turns out okay in early Y2K tests across USA. *Family Weekly's* survey has the three biggest stories in the past century — "Man on Moon," "Pearl Harbor Attack," and the "Sinking of the Titanic."

October 14, 1999 — Most Americans won't travel on New Year's Eve. Nearly two-thirds of Americans are not very likely to take a vacation to start 2000. However just five percent cited worries about computer snafus as the reason. They just want to wait and see what happens.

December 9, 1999 — I started emergency boxes for our kids for Christmas. I printed humorous Y2K cards (showing a person in the basement with a clock reading ten minutes to midnight, cans piled everywhere and a cartoon character with a scuba breathing tube in his mouth). I taped this to the front of the wrapped open box and filled it with goodies! You never know when a can of Pringles will save the day.

December 24, 1999 — Newspapers are saying to get your books Y2K-ready. If the power does go out, the theaters and video stores will be closed. It pays to be prepared; you'll need to curl up with a candle or a flashlight and a good book. Some of the titles out there now are racing up the bestseller lists as we try to make sense of it all: *Life: Our Century in Pictures,* from the magazine's photo archives, and *The Century.*

December 30, 1999 — Because our century is coming to an end, the newspapers are filled with all sorts of fascinating stories from the past hundred years.

January 1, 2000 — As 2000 began, the news was filled with coverage of each time zone from all over the world. The Eiffel Tower was lit up beautifully, and in London Big Ben chimed while a huge fireworks show filled the skies. Times Square had a live celebration with a Waterford glass ball dropping as 2000 rang in.

A humorous cartoon in our newspaper summed up everything. As far as I know, none of these things really happened.

"Y2K Disaster — Was the Wait Worth It?"
"5 ATM Machines Fail to Work Properly!"
"Power Out to Over 3 Homes in Northeast!"
"Not All Library Cards Are Recognized!"
"Automatic Toilet Won't Stop Flushing!"
"Terrified Residents in Dark 7 Minutes!"

My Leaving Machine Is Well-Oiled...

Ruth Sabath Rosenthal

and I've a niggling notion to set it
in motion – the contraption made fit
for the long haul by a hearty infusion
of a freshly-rendered vitriol solution.

A swine, long driving me to wine
and rant over his mounting two-timing,
has thinned my taut-as-wire smile
to the verge of snapping. What guile!

I'm leaving! Off this ache-rage in my trusty tractor,
in search of that green pasture
far from the weed field this wilderness is
where the only seeds tilled are foolish wishes,

I'll hug the road till I find an orchard filled
with fruit just ripe for the picking – and I will.

Waiting on Hold

Penny Righthand

You are waiting on hold for the irritating music to end – someone's idea of what will keep you entertained and willing to wait an inordinate amount of time for the next robotic voice or (if you're fortunate) for the next human (who may or may not speak the same language as you) to ask you how they can give you excellent service today. You glance at your computer screen sitting on your desk in front of you. For some reason you have the thought that, after twenty years, your assistant still calls it a computer "scream" much like your five-year-old grandson calls his skeleton costume a "stellakin." Your mind is desperate for entertaining thoughts.

Your eyes settle on the screen which distracts you from the music that annoys you, and you get absorbed in replying to email messages which require your attention anyway, and you congratulate yourself for one brief second on how at least you aren't wasting time, when you think you hear the click on the phone indicating someone has picked up. In your haste you inadvertently touch the "send" button on the screen instead of the "talk" button on the phone, and you send a message you weren't quite ready to send, having just had the thought that it sounded a little strident. Of course, you realize there is no "unsend" button, stirring in you a memory you recognize as one left over from the days of a prior technological breakthrough, the phone answering machine, when you'd left a message you really wish you hadn't left. And, perhaps, you think, that feeling goes back even farther to a time when it wasn't even technology's failure to retrieve a message you mistakenly sent, but the failure of your own mouth to stay shut until your thoughts were well enough thought out to avoid ending that first marriage unnecessarily. You realize this some forty years too late, having left a later marriage for a somewhat better reason, and finding yourself alone now with a computer and an iPhone (your best and most meaningful relationship yet, you'd thought, until Apple found a way to have your iPhone talk back to you).

"Hello," you hear on your phone which has been on speaker while you multitasked so everyone else around could suffer the music, which you suddenly realize, is the *Nutcracker Suite*, still playing in July.

In your rush to switch the phone back to your earpiece, you hear "hello" again; you say "hello" yourself, rapidly, repeatedly, loudly, as you try to recover the receiver which has momentarily slipped from your fingers...and a voice with an accent you work hard to understand asks you that fatal question, "How can I give you excellent service today?"

You have to rein in your urge to tell her that changing the music to something more seasonal would be a good first step, and that being on hold for eleven minutes is too long, but you manage to merely make the request you called about, though it takes you a moment to even remember what that was.

And then she tells you, after all, that she cannot help you with your problem; but she will be "ever so happy to connect you with the appropriate department. And please let me give you the phone number in case we get disconnected. And would you like to take the short survey at the end of your call?"

You write down the number, though she has to repeat it since it's hard to find a pen and paper in your high-tech office. She tells you to have a wonderful day, which you suspect is scripted, and you sense is unlikely, at best. Then you hear the "click" indicating that she has disconnected you. You are on your own again when you notice there is already an answer to your ill-sent email – not a promising sign, you think, wishing you could slam the phone down in frustration, but all you can do is touch the button on the screen that says "end call."

She Was Eighty-Three

Martha O'Quinn

The call comes late in the evening,
Mama hospitalized, breath labored.
Rushing to her side I long to hear
recovery in progress. Instead,
heart failing, kidneys shutting down;
twenty-four hours at most.
Three weeks crawl by.
Enclosed with impending death
my own mortality becomes real.
She can probably hear, they say.
I ramble, speak to her of happy times.
Twenty-four/seven I sit and wait. Why?
For peace of mind and to ease
my guilt from inattention in the past.
She's so vulnerable, her eyes squeezed tight
under the bright lights over her bed.
She's had eye surgery, can't tolerate light, I say.
She's not aware of light, I'm told.
If she can hear she is aware of light.
Angrily I turn them off.
She wishes to die. I give my permission.
Each day brings new signs;
the end is near. Still I wait

process of becoming what God wants us to be." John Ortberg ~§~

and still she breathes.
Let it be over I pray.
The hospital can no longer give palliative care.
A nursing home looms.
Her final morning dawns. Answered prayers.
She draws one last breath.
I exit the cold and clinical,
warmed with memories of her love.

In memory of my mother who died May 1, 1996.

Storm Front

Renee Emerson

I listen to rain falling down the chimney,
rattling like bracelets on a bony arm.
The wind sucks out air
from the house, making the sound of fire
where there is no fire.
I am on our red couch writing;
you are in the bedroom sleeping.
If the storm comes, it will come
for us both, writing or sleeping,
so I let you sleep, the better way
to meet fate: with your eyes closed
thinking of something else.

"Teach us, O Lord, the disciplines of patience, for to wait is often

Still Hoping

Carol McAdoo Rehme

I simply want a sign
Last brilliant leaf on a windblown tree
Butterflies in winter
Shiny penny in a muddy gutter
Words across a billboard
Our initials carved into a stump

I simply need a sign

The pungent whiff of Ben Gay
Love letters left on my pillow
My name whispered in a familiar way
Your shadow splayed on the bedroom floor
Your silly fishing hat bobbing in a crowd
"Bye Bye Miss American Pie" drifting from a car radio
An anonymous bouquet of sunny roses waiting at
    the stoop
A single brilliant blue feather drifting from the
    heavens

One
vivid
dream

I'm waiting. For a sign

The Floor Moved a Little

Carly Berg

"A breast needle biopsy is a minor procedure, Mrs. Jackson," the nurse told me over the phone.

"We do them right here in the office."

The floor seemed to move a little under my feet as I told my husband about it.

Later that evening, *Hoarders* was on and I was too lazy to get up. "Would you bring me a Sprite with ice, Honey?" I called to him.

"Would you bring yourself a Sprite with ice, Honey?" He was playing his stupid computer game.

"Never mind," I said, not really thinking. "I'll just die."

He began to cry.

I felt godawful terrible. I hugged his head to my chest. At the same time, I was about to fall over laughing, because I am an idiot.

Three days later, we were in the waiting room. Someone had attached two felt Santa hats to the coffee cart, holiday decorations. I thought about caffeine causing breast lumps, but got a cup anyway.

A tiny Asian man yanked at the pointy red hats. "They yours? They yours?" We said no, but he didn't understand. He seemed perplexed that he could not pick up the hats we had forgotten. He wanted to return them to us. The man yanked. The coffee cart shook.

My husband and I snickered behind our hands. "You are so bad," I told him.

I finished filling out the forms, returned the clipboard to the girl at the desk. I swiped the pen, though. My husband would think it was funny.

We talked about lunch. Right after this we'd go to our favorite seafood joint and get everything we felt like getting – who cared what it cost.

An elderly woman was up at the front desk. She talked on and on, one of those old people who think the medical staff are their friends. The woman had on a black beret, black slacks, black coat. She was heavyset, the same thickness all the way up and down. "Look, Honey," I whispered to my husband. "It's a phone booth. Not many of those around anymore."

His eyes widened in mock horror. "God's gonna get you for that."

I cracked up, swallowed my coffee wrong, coughed.

"There now, see? That's what you get."

After filling in an answer in my crossword book, I passed it and the illicit pen to my husband. "Your turn. They sure do take their time here."

The old woman in black clumped by with her cane. "Look," my husband whispered, "it's the angel of death."

"Oh, you're evil."
We howled into our hands.
"Mrs. Jackson?" the doctor's assistant called.
We stopped laughing. I stood up. The old woman nodded, and the floor moved a little under my feet.

Little March's Gift

Steliana Cristina Voicu

White and red freesias laugh at the window,
but their joy I cannot hear
since I am waiting for hospital news —
o, longest hours! —
the time divides as a fractal
while I am waiting for my sister to give birth.
The phone rings...my mom cannot speak,
but her eyes speak for her...

Her first grandchild is a *mărţişor**
from 1200 kilometers away...

*Mărţişor: Romanian, "Little March's gift"

The Beginnings of Grief
Deborah Straw

"When your father dies,
I'll want to die,"
my mother tells me,
as we ride in the country

on a gray autumn day.

Ten years his junior,
at seventy-six,
she's vital, bored, lonely.

Yet, attached,
so attached to Dad,
like she might have been to her mother,
had she stayed home longer,
like she might have been to me,
had I lived nearby longer.

Under-stimulated,
she spends her days
watering plants,
watching soaps,
reading mysteries,

worrying and nagging my dad,
feeding him, fixing his buttons,
keeping him warm.

At eighty-six,
he's in good health.
A bit thin;
he's down to boys' shirts.
A bit frail;
he's using a cane.

But his mind and his will
are strong.
He has more humor and despair
than physical energy.

Yet, I constantly steel myself
for the call I could receive
at any time, any day.

His irregular heart could give out.
So could my mother,
this woman who
has taught me
so many ways to be,
and not to be,
a woman and a wife.

~§~ *"Let us not be content to wait and see what will happen, but give*

Red-Tape Rhumba

Mary Carter

Though progress and prosperity are grand,
a dreadful malady their spread attends:
Technology, our servant, sadly lends
itself to this great blight upon our land.

Few businesses these days are fully manned.
Instead of human contact we may get
recorded messages and music set
to "serve" the patrons tortures of the damned.

How many useless hours have I spent...
not contemplating truth or beauty rare,
not searching for the storied pot of gold,
but wading through a menu's labyrinth?
Oh, I could be the grandest millionaire
with a nickel for each minute spent "on hold."

Escape

Nancy Gauquier

It was the early '60s, and I'd finally graduated and escaped the small town in New England where I grew up. I was wandering around Times Square on a sunny afternoon. I was elated even though I was broke, high on the fact that I was actually in New York City. I stopped to gaze at a movie poster for a Shirley MacLaine movie. I was wearing my looking-for-a-job outfit, a blouse with a short skirt and my only pair of pantyhose that didn't have a run.

"Want to see that?"

I glanced around and there was a man in his thirties, in a business suit. His face didn't tell me anything. What did he want? He looked so impersonal he was a little scary, but I wanted to see this movie, and I was broke.

"No strings?"

"Not if you don't want."

"I don't."

"Okay."

I shrugged.

He paid my way and we entered the lobby and climbed the stairs and sat beside each other in the middle of the theater. He never said a word, but as soon as the movie started, his hand was on my knee, and moving up. I grabbed it and it stopped, but I couldn't lift it off, it was too heavy. He wouldn't let go. When I let go of his hand, it started moving up again. He was stiff and looked straight ahead, he didn't even turn his head, as if it had nothing to do with him; he had no idea what his hand was doing. This was not good.

I got up. "I have to go to the bathroom." I made my way out to the aisle, whispering "Excuse me" to the disgruntled people I was stumbling over.

I sat in one of the very back rows. He'd never find me. I was just getting back into the movie when I felt the hand on my knee again. I glanced over and it was him, looking straight ahead like a statue. How did he find me in the dark? He didn't say a word. There were definitely strings. Now I was freaked.

"Excuse me."

I found my way to the very back of the theater, and on the side there was a lit EXIT sign above a door. I wanted out fast. I slipped out and shut the door behind me.

I was free! I was out of there!

Then I turned around.

Wait a minute. I was on a fire escape. A very high fire escape and there was no way down. I was on this very small fire escape balcony, and it felt very flimsy, just steel bars...

I turned back around to open the door, but it wouldn't budge. It was locked. You could get out but you couldn't get back in. It was a thick, heavy, soundproof door.

I was so high up the people below looked like little animations. I kept trying the door. I couldn't believe it. It had to open, but it wouldn't budge. I knocked and yelled but no one could hear me. I kicked it and almost broke my foot.

I was trapped on a fire escape above Times Square. Nobody ever came out there. Nobody else would have any reason to. They'd find my skeleton in rags in about ten years, when they had their next fire drill. And I didn't even get to see the movie. My mother would wonder why I never wrote, not even for money.

I looked down, but that was not a good idea; my perch was old and precarious. I was not fond of heights; I got dizzy, and there was a lot of space between the bars. I backed into a corner and held on.

No one was going to notice me way up there, even if they did look up. Not many people walked by below as the fire escape was over an alleyway.

I pounded on the door until my fists were sore, but it was futile.

"Help!" I was too embarrassed to yell loudly. Besides, no one could hear me.

The sun would go down and no one would see me. My stomach started to rumble and I thought of the deli coleslaw in my musty old hotel room, but the cockroaches would get to it before I did. They were probably cracking open the lid right then.

I fished a pen and a small notebook out of my bag, wrote, "Help! I'm trapped on the fire escape!" and dropped the little slips of paper to the sidewalk, whenever I caught sight of a passer-by. I kept tearing out pages and littering the alleyway below. They drifted down at an unbearably slow rate, and landed on the sidewalk behind the people who had already moved on.

"Please, God, just let me out of here and I'll never do this again." I felt like an idiot in a cage. I wished I could die, but not slowly of starvation on a fire escape above Times Square, so I kept dropping the little white fluttering papers that skittered out of sight.

My mother would never report me missing; she didn't believe in bothering the police about family stuff. And even if she could afford a private detective, it was unlikely he'd think of searching every movie theater fire escape in New York City. By the time they found me, they wouldn't even be able to identify me by my teeth. The first inkling anyone would have would be when my bones slipped through the steel bars and hit someone below on the head.

How come no one ever warned me about the dangers of New York City fire escapes? How come nobody ever took me aside and said, "Look, Honey, don't ever close a door until you know where you are." Nobody ever told me that even an exit sign can be misleading.

I dropped a note and it wafted its way down to the concrete sidewalk, and landed safely, unmolested, right after the stroller had walked by, as if it had no intention of ever alerting anyone.

I kept tossing notes – I couldn't think of anything else to do – until finally – *finally* – someone saw one and glanced up.

I pointed to the note.

He chased it, got it, read it and looked up again.

I was madly gesticulating. *Help!*

And then he was gone.

He glanced up, and then he was gone. Maybe he thought I was crazy.

Maybe he thought it was some kind of a joke.

And then – nothing.

It was getting later and later. I was afraid I'd have to spend the whole night on that fire escape. And then how many nights? It was getting colder, and what if I fell asleep and rolled over and plummeted to the concrete faster than any slip of paper?

No one else was walking by. I huddled in the corner by the wall, and stared down at the sidewalk until – finally – the door opened behind me – and there were five curious men in blue.

I had to explain everything to the cops, as they escorted me through the theater and down the stairs laughing, and out into the anonymous release of an early evening in New York.

November 22, 1911

Martha O'Quinn

He clicks his tongue, slaps reins
across the mules' haunches,
begins his trip to where she waits.
He's twenty, unaware of
frigid temperatures. He smiles.
She paces, pauses to peer
from behind a muslin curtain
hanging from wire suspended
between two nails.
She's eighteen, she trembles.
He speaks to the team of mules,
vapor from frosty breath
seems suspended in mid-air.
They rear heads, hooves paw in protest.
She listens in disbelief to Mother,
her eyes plead for reassurance.
He pats his inside coat pocket,
feels the crinkle of paper and
a lump – the ring. He smiles.
She hears wagon wheels creak,
mules snort. She trembles.
Mother nods her head, opens the door.
He jumps from the wagon seat,

~§~ "They also serve who only stand and wait." John Milton ~§~

she hands him her clothing satchel
and a cardboard box, secured with twine.
She climbs onto the wagon,
they journey across the field that leads
to the minister's home. He smiles.
She stares straight ahead, appears comatose
as she tries to erase the mental picture
formed from her mother's words...
events yet to occur on her wedding night.

Thawing Ground

Renee Emerson

A cool wind, the final
remark of winter.
White azaleas
in the half-light lull
of the evening.
The linden trees shudder.
I wrap my coat tight
against the swell
of my belly and think
to next year's spring
when our child will feel
for the first time
the warmth the world
can carry, and, afterward,
its long withholding.

"Things may come to those who wait, but only the things left by those

Waiting after a Blizzard

Patricia Podlipec

Snow, like a chrysalis,
wraps my garden.
White, too, encases me,
but I fail to emulate
sleeping plants awaiting
the busy season ahead.

Instead I flutter
        from window
to window
        seeking escape

to the world outside where
appointments and commitments
will bring longing,
once again, for dormancy.

Winning Life's Waiting Game
Francine Baldwin-Billingslea

It took more years than I care to count before finally learning and understanding that waiting is a part of life we just can't change. Whatever we go through, whatever we want or whatever we need, waiting is definitely going to be involved. It didn't matter how much I cried or tried to rush things, I always had to wait. Then, of course, there were things I felt that I just couldn't wait for, but didn't have a choice but to wait for: those much hoped-for manifestations.

I waited for the man of my dreams, the birth of my child, and for the right job to come along. I waited for my home to get built, the results of a traumatic medical diagnosis and for health and healing to come. I've waited for that dress, shoes or stove to go on sale. I've impatiently waited for prescriptions to get filled, for my number to be called while playing bingo or for that extremely long traffic light to change. I've waited for retirement and now that it's here, I wait for my monthly check. The list goes on and on and there's not a day that goes by that we don't have to wait for something.

There have been times that, as I waited for things, I cried, cussed, fussed, threw tantrums, walked the floor, tossed and turned in bed all night. Or I tried to give a helping hand, hoping to rush the process, answers or solutions, only to find out that all of the above were done in vain and only caused additional stress. I absolutely hated waiting for anything and yet, I had to wait for everything. I often found myself agitated and anxious. However, I realized the hard way that this wasn't a healthy way to conduct my life and steer my energy, nor did it help matters as I often sat in the holding patterns in the "Waiting Game" of life. Since I couldn't change this irritating facet of persistent existence, I had to change how I waited. But first I had to realize that things weren't always going to go my way when and how I wanted them to go. Second, I had to realize that I couldn't worry or stress over things that were beyond my control. Third, I just had to accept that waiting is a part of life. I had to learn to wait in a more positive way and without the tantrums.

Nightwatchman

Janina Aza Karpinska

He waits – in the dark – of the kitchenette
as she creeps in through the back door
long after midnight.

She notices his steeple of fingers —
pressed up against his lips
as though in prayer.

Nothing will happen as long as
these hands keep this shape
as they barricade his mouth. But

she's unable to trust that cough —
like the sound of strained rope
that's about to give.

I don't think I mind waiting because
Judy Callarman

I know someday my balance will come.
Mother said so, and I believe her.
Adults, I see, are sure of themselves.
As one, I will have it all together,
declare an end to all this fearful stuff.

> *'Tis the gift to be simple, 'tis the gift to be free*
> *'Tis the gift to come down where we ought to be*

Free at last, I will be able to talk to boys,
to look into curious eyes of strangers,
know how to act and how to dress
and walk into a room of seated Others.

> *And when we find ourselves in the place just right,*
> *'Twill be in the valley of love and delight.*

And then One will love me as I am,
see my soft heart and tender feelings,
know me as I have never been known.

> *When true simplicity is gain'd,*
> *To bow and to bend we shan't be asham'd*

True Love will save me from myself
and inside and outside will be the same —

To turn, turn will be our delight,
Till by turning, turning we come 'round right

if I can just wait that long.

    * In its original form, "Simple Gifts" is a one-verse Quaker dance song written in 1846 by Elder Joseph Brackett.

On Yet Another Birthday
Ruth Sabath Rosenthal

my prized micro-cassette
i keep stashed away
in my dresser drawer
but for this day
each year when i take it
out of its velvet-lined box
to play and replay
my father's message
promising he'll return
my call soon
as possible

Haiku Hannah

mile one hundred
two-day trip with toddlers
are we there yet?

Haiku Hannah

longest second
at parabola's zenith
roller coaster

Haiku Hannah

anxiety gap
from novocain injection
to totally numb

Calling Home

Alice King Greenwood

I jumped up quickly at the shrill ringing of the telephone and ran to answer it. At 11:15 p.m. the news might be very good or very bad. Apprehensive, I picked up the phone, almost dreading to hear the message.

* * *

It was mid-afternoon when my husband, Morris, got in our pickup truck to run an errand at the mall, which was just three blocks away. "I'll be home in a few minutes," he said. "Just need to pay this bill and I'll be right back."

"All right. I'll have supper ready soon," I called as he drove out the driveway.

At 4:30 traffic was very heavy on our city's most-traveled street, which ran alongside the mall. After half an hour had passed, I began to get anxious. Morris was a diabetic, and although he took unusually good care of himself and ate his meals on time, his blood sugars were erratic. They sometimes plummeted without warning. He had had hypoglycemic reactions in which he lost consciousness, but when I was with him I could recognize the onset of the symptoms and give him quick-acting glucose, usually orange juice, to remedy the problem.

This afternoon, though, he was feeling fine when he left home, and he would not be gone long. But as a half hour stretched into an hour, then two, my anxiety turned to worry. Then panic. My imagination began to run wild. Had he been in a wreck? What if he had been robbed, knocked out and left injured somewhere? What if he had been killed? There had been two murders in our city in recent weeks.

Not having another car, I could not go looking for him myself. I called our two sons-in-law and some friends, who hurried over to the mall. When they could not find our truck in the parking lot, they began combing the streets. Every thirty minutes or so, one of them called to report on the situation or to ask if he had been located. Each call brought first hope, then disappointment, as time after time the reports were not positive. I called the police department so they, too, could be on the lookout for him. I hoped they would take my report seriously and not think this was just another case of a husband not coming home to his wife.

By now three hours had passed. It was long past supper time, so I knew that even if he had not been harmed, his blood sugar would be getting very low. I was frantic. I called other relatives and friends, some living in distant cities, and they, in turn, spread the word to their praying friends.

upon the LORD shall renew their strength; they shall mount up with

From the beginning of the ordeal I had been praying fervently for God's protection and that Morris would be found unharmed. I had always thought I could handle emergency situations in a calm manner, but now I was nervous. Home alone, and watching the hours tick by, I found it was not easy to think rationally when one's mind is paralyzed by fear. I reached out for a word from God.

I had memorized many Scriptures, but initially it was hard to recall the specific passages I needed. Gradually, though, one after another came to mind. "Call unto me and I will answer thee, and show thee great and mighty things which thou knowest not" (Jeremiah 33:3). "Thou wilt keep him in perfect peace whose mind is stayed on thee, because he trusteth in thee" (Isaiah 26:3). I picked up my Bible and began reading some of the Psalms. God's presence became real as I sensed His calming assurance. "Do you not know that I am in control, that Morris' life is in my hands?" He seemed to say. "Haven't I always kept my promises to care for you? Don't you remember the many times I have answered your prayers in the past?" Yes, I remembered, and I was filled with a resurgence of hope

* * *

Morris finished his errand at the mall, walked out to the parking lot and climbed into his pickup. Automatically, he turned on the ignition and pulled out, slowly, into the rush-hour traffic. He followed the busy street five miles, six miles, across town before turning left, all the while driving more slowly with each passing minute.

The road to the left continued out of town and became a highway to the little town of Crane, thirty miles away. The highway was under construction. Heavy road equipment was parked for the night on either side. Road signs and orange barrels warned of uneven lanes and other driving hazards.

The sun set. Morris drove on.

Some hours later, lying in the truck in a ditch along the road, he gradually became aware he was in the open country because he could hear the sound of pump jacks in the oil fields. Rallying just enough to realize his blood sugar was low, he ate a piece of hard candy which he always carried in his pocket. Then he started the engine and pulled up onto the road.

Passing in and out of consciousness and not knowing where the highway led, he continued to drive. A while later, a highway sign came into view indicating the town of Crane, just a few miles ahead. Now he knew where he was.

At that late hour only a Seven-Eleven convenience store was still open. He stopped in the parking lot and went inside. "Ma'am," he managed to say to the clerk, "I'm having trouble and I need help. Could you give me some orange juice?"

and not faint." Isaiah 40:31 ~§~ "My observation is that women are

"Sure, Mister," she replied as she pulled out a carton from the refrigerator. "Are you sick?"

"I think my blood sugar is low. I'm diabetic."

"Oh. Then do you want to call home? Here, you can use my phone."

Morris drank the carton dry and picked up the phone, but in his befuddled mind he could not remember his phone number. Turning to the clerk again, he asked her to call the police for help.

In a few minutes the sole policeman on duty in Crane pulled up the store.

"Having trouble, are you, Mister? Let me see your driver's license and I'll help you notify your family," he kindly offered. After locating the name and address, he found the phone number listed in the telephone directory, dialed it, and handed the phone to Morris.

* * *

When my phone rang at 11:15 – seven hours after he left home – Morris was on the line.

"I'm okay," he said, his voice weak. "I'm in Crane. Can you come get me? The policeman will stay with me until you get here."

My son-in-law and I drove the thirty miles to Crane in record time. We pulled into the Seven-Eleven, helped Morris into the car, profusely thanked the clerk and policeman who had helped him, and brought him safely home at last.

We felt as though we had just witnessed a real miracle. Only God's hand could have guided him through the heavy traffic and torn-up highway, protecting him from accident and injury to himself and others. God brought him out of unconsciousness when normally, over time, he would have gone deeper into a coma and possibly death. Through that harrowing experience, we learned anew to trust God completely. He was in control.

To Jillian, at Midnight

Melody Mann

You couldn't wait to show me
    All your latest backyard finds.

You couldn't wait to tell me
    What was freshly on your mind.

You couldn't wait to grow up
    And leave childish things behind.

You couldn't bear to slow up;
    Now you're never home on time.

Waiting for the Next Move

Wayne Faust

Bobby stared at the chessboard. Joseph had stepped out in the middle of the game, going to investigate a noise from up above, and he still hadn't returned. In the meantime, Bobby was analyzing every possible move that Joseph could make.

Bobby didn't know or care what was making the quiet humming noise inside the walls. Smells didn't faze him either, good or bad. He didn't care what the temperature was. He never looked up at the clock on the mantle, nor did he notice it counting the seconds, the hours, the days. He cared only about the game in front of him.

A mouse scampered across the floor, its nose like a vacuum cleaner. Bobby didn't mind the mice, for they never sniffed him. To them, he might as well have been part of the chair.

He thought of some of the things that Joseph had taught him. "Don't be so hasty," he had once said. "Even if you know what move you're gonna make, it's best to wait a little while. Let your opponent think you're worried. Besides, when you make

a move two seconds after I do it really ticks me off."
And then Joseph had laughed.

So Bobby had learned to be patient. He didn't
want to make Joseph angry, because if that hap-
pened, then he might not want to play anymore.
And then what?

Bobby focused. There were a lot of moves that
Joseph could make. Bishop to c4...knight to h4...
queen to g6...And on and on.

The moves cascaded through Bobby's brain,
along with all the countermoves that Joseph could
make. And then there were countermoves to those.
The possibilities grew exponentially, but Bobby was
determined to map them all out, so that when
Joseph came back, whatever move he made
wouldn't matter and Bobby would win.

Because Bobby was a player.

* * *

A loud, muffled thud came from the ceiling
above. A cascade of dirt and plaster fell into the
center of the room. A hole opened up and bright
sunlight shone down through the stale air.

Bobby looked up from the chessboard.
"Joseph?" he called.

"There's something here!" cried a voice from
above.

A few minutes later, a rope came down through
the hole. Two figures climbed down, a man and a
woman. They brushed themselves off and gazed
open-mouthed at the pictures on the wall, the single

cot, and the food boxes stacked floor to ceiling. They turned their gazes toward Bobby, sitting at his table and his chessboard.

"Where's Joseph?" asked Bobby.

"What?" asked the man, who was tall, and much younger than Joseph.

"It is Joseph's move."

The man paused for a long moment. Then he and the woman whispered back and forth among themselves. Finally, they approached, stepping around the fallen dirt and pieces of ceiling. The sunlight from above back-lit their faces so Bobby couldn't see what they looked like.

"Will Joseph come back soon?" asked Bobby.

The man reached out to touch one of the pieces on the chessboard.

"Do not touch that!" said Bobby sharply. "It is Joseph's move."

The man glanced at his companion. Then he looked down at Bobby. "Joseph is gone," he said softly.

"I know that," answered Bobby. "When will he come back?"

The man sighed. "Joseph is dead."

Bobby laughed. "Joseph uses that word when he knows he will soon be checkmated. 'I am dead,' he says."

The man looked at his companion, and shrugged. Now the woman spoke. "It means that

Joseph is never coming back again," she said. "Not ever."

"But he didn't finish the game," said Bobby.

"Joseph died a very long time ago. Seventy-five years at least. During the Wars. But I guess that must seem like yesterday to you."

"I do not understand," said Bobby, frowning.

The woman examined the chessboard for a few moments. "No wonder old Joseph ran off," she muttered. "Checkmate in five moves."

She turned to her companion. "This is one of the early Bobby Fisher Models," she said. "My grandpa had one just like it. Taught me to play. I always loved his eyes, so expressive, like a lost puppy. When I was little, I thought he was a real person. He kept me company. I didn't have a lot of friends in those days."

"We have to go," said her companion.

"Give us a few minutes," she said.

"But..." sputtered the man, "we're supposed to..."

"I know," she answered. "It won't be long."

The man mumbled under his breath and drifted over to a far corner of the room.

The woman turned back to Bobby. "My name is Louise," she said. "You must be Bobby."

"Yes."

"Well, Bobby, Joseph wanted me to tell you he's sorry that he couldn't make it back. He asked me to finish the game for him. Is that okay?"

"But..." said Bobby.

"I'm sure I'm not as good a player as Joseph, but I'll try my best."

"Very well."

Louise pulled up a rusty folding chair and sat down. She was at Bobby's level now so he could see her better. He liked her face, especially her eyes.

"It is your move," said Bobby.

"Yep," said Louise. Under her breath she muttered, "I sure hope this is a good idea."

Bishop to c4.

Bobby knew the counter move, for he had been thinking about it for a long, long time. But Joseph had taught him to be patient. He whistled softly and grunted a few times. "Nice day," he said.

"Yes, it is," answered Louise.

At last, Bobby made his move.

Knight takes pawn.

Bobby wondered if Louise knew the trap she was getting herself into. Checkmate in four moves.

As Louise stared at the dusty, yellowed game board, Bobby planned his opening move for the next game.

Waiting for a Reply

J.J. Steinfeld

three or four words
that break the sadness
not all that much to request

fill out the form
hand it in
wait for a reply

I've been waiting here
for longer than I can remember
the room overcrowded

fill out the form
hand it in
wait for a reply

I understand there have been errors
a name misspelled, a number inaccurate
the intricacies of sadness abundant

fill out the form
hand it in
wait for a reply

"The folly of not waiting for God is that we forfeit the blessing of hav-

how about one word
that fools the sadness
not all that much to request

fill out the form
hand it in
wait for a reply

is that why you're so sad
having to deal with people like me
making unreasonable requests?

fill out the form
hand it in
wait for a reply

forgotten magic words

Carl Palmer

formal invitation
graduation announcement

first communication since
elementary school written

in his mother's handwriting
check sent check cashed

time passes

Biopsy

Shawn Aveningo

I wait for the phone to ring,
realizing that a call this soon
couldn't be good news.
Results never rushed,
without reason.

I taste the biscuits and gravy
my girls prepared for
Mother's Day.

I feel the arms of my son
wrapped around me
before he returned to campus.

I recall the warmth of the sun
as I bathe in its radiance,
my dogs licking my knee pits,
protecting me from overexposure.

My mind launches me
to simpler days with my sister,
running through sprinklers,
chasing lightning bugs,
building forts from lawn chairs and
sheets we stole from the clothesline.

I can hear the purr of Sunshine
my round-bellied cat, nuzzling
under my neck as I napped.

I cry
as I remember the exquisite beauty
of love we made,
hoping it wasn't the last.

Ring... Ring... Ring... Ring.

Hurry and Wait...

Elsi Dodge

Dentist's office, doctor's door —
If you're early, wait some more.
Minutes passing...what a bore!
I'll read while waiting; let's begin.

This book and I, we've got a date,
And I'll be glad to sit and wait!
Oh, no – a twist of joking fate:
"We're ready now! Walk right on in!"

The Wait Is Killing Me

Dare Freeman Ford

We travel hours
to consult doctors
who hold our futures
like bubbles above briars.

Seeking respite
from our bodies' betrayals
we crave remissions, cures.

Elevator doors open
spill us like marbles
scattering across the floor.

Young, old, and in-between,
in wheelchairs, on walkers,
in face masks, hauling oxygen,
we wait.

In silence
we hang,
entangled in the system
like flies in a web.

And Then She Died...

Kat Bert

Jennifer watched as Ben lotioned his wife's hands. The touch was tender. Intimate. She tried to turn away as one by one gentle kisses caressed his Virginia's fingertips. She felt intrusive, but she was there to help. She had become a fixture in their home. This was just one of many moments she had been privileged to observe.

"She's asleep," Ben said with oppressive weariness. This man was losing his wife. Five months ago he had asked for hospice, and now he was hanging on to her life with the determination of every man who had ever lost his wife.

"She's breathing a little easier," Jennifer said. She put her stethoscope in her bag. The small tasks of her day made her job a little easier. She was used to death; she'd been a hospice nurse for years – too many to count – but this was a hard one. She had come to care for this family. Boundaries were hard to adhere to with Ben and Virginia. She couldn't explain it. Sometimes it just happened that way.

"I'll go get us some tea," Ben said as he shuffled out of the room. When he returned with two china

can become spiritually spastic, trying to make the right things happen

cups, each delicate and cherished, he offered one to Jennifer. She took it, noticing again how tired Ben looked. He was old, yes, and looked the way a man should look after he'd walked through his life for 78 years, but until recently there were remnants of handsome years that played around the corners of his eyes. Today he just looked tired, his looks now lost in the passing of daily living, of raising a family, watching them grow and leave, and in caring for his loved wife.

Ben had been dealing with Virginia as a hospice patient for five months now, but the last two days had been hard. Reality was crashing in on him. For the first time, today he was realizing that dying meant it was time for her to die. His wife. His beloved Virginia.

Jennifer raised the proffered cup to her lips. She wasn't sure what she was drinking. Tea, Ben had called it, but it was a watered-down version, perhaps a left-over habit Virginia had taught him: saving the "good stuff" in case it was needed later.

"Do you think she's in pain?" Ben asked, the weariness of his question bending his form into a chair.

"She's not in pain right now," Jennifer said.

"You know this?" Ben's question was filled with a doubtful hope. He had seen Virginia through years of pain.

"She isn't grimacing," Virginia said. "She's comfortable." She looked again at Virginia. Her face was peaceful. Vacant, but peaceful. "Do you mind if I sit down?" she asked as she reached for a chair.

"I'm sorry, I should have offered." Ben raised the cup to his lips, but failed to take a drink.

Jennifer sat down, "Tell me about her." She leaned in close to him, took the stilled cup from his hands and set it on the dresser beside Virginia's bed. She already knew a lot about Virginia's life, her likes and dislikes, how they'd met; but Ben needed to talk, to say something other than the words that she could see screaming behind his worried brow – my wife is dying!

He stayed silent.

Jennifer sat back in her chair; she reached out with the practiced hand of a thirty-year veteran to stroke her patient's leg. A low hum rose from her throat, an Irish lullaby Ben had taught her months ago. It was one of Virginia's favorites.

She watched as Ben raised his eyes to her.

"What will happen..." he began but stopped. His eyes filled with tears.

"Ben," Jennifer took his hands in hers, "Ask me anything. I'll tell you the truth."

For a long time he said nothing. When he finally did speak, his voice was clear and strong. Jennifer hadn't expected that.

"What will happen tonight?"

"She may die tonight." It always sounded so harsh when she said those words, but they were the truth and she had promised she would be honest.

"I've never seen anyone die." The quake in his voice almost imperceptible, but heartbreaking.

"It can be very peaceful." Jennifer looked at her patient; Virginia wasn't there anymore to anyone but Ben.

"Will it be for her?"

"We will do our best for her," Jennifer again promised.

"Is it quiet?"

"It can be," Jennifer said. "She's likely to just stop breathing. Virginia has been quiet for days now."

"I know," Ben said, as he reached for his wife's hand. His thumb caressed the ring she'd worn for sixty years. "She'll stop breathing and then she'll..." He couldn't bring himself to say the words.

"She will die." Jennifer didn't flinch. Her voice didn't break. This was her job. She was trained to give it straight. To say, "she'll be okay" to the husband of a hospice patient was unfair, cruel. It bordered on professional irresponsibility.

"She will die," Ben said. The tears that welled in his eyes never fell. "I want to say so many things to her." He wiped a weary hand across his face. "I want to tell her how much I love her, how much I'll miss her." His hand continued to caress her fingers. He leaned in to kiss her hand one more time. "I want to ask her not to go," he said. A tear finally rolled down his cheek.

"You can tell her how much you love her," Jennifer said. "You can tell her how much you'll miss her, but don't ask her to stay." Jennifer leaned in a little closer, "She wants to, Ben, but she can't and you don't want her to feel like she's disappointed you."

Ben looked at Jennifer, "She's never disappointed me a day in her life," he said, his voice faltering. "She's been the love of my life, my June bug."

"But she's tired."

"And now she's dying."

"Yes," Jennifer said. "And now she's dying."

The low lullaby again rose from Jennifer's throat. She leaned back in her chair and waited a few minutes. Virginia's rest was peaceful. It was time for Jennifer to step out of the room. She owed it to them to give them a few minutes alone. Years of experience told her Virginia's death would likely be tonight. She watched as Ben spoke inaudible words into Virginia's cheek punctuated with tender kisses.

She was about to leave when she heard a slow sigh escape from Virginia. The nurse in her told her to stay, maybe a minute or two more. Sometimes just a low song and a light touch would soothe a patient back into peaceful sleep. With the instinct of thirty years she put down her bag as she heard a very small voice try to speak. She looked over at Virginia, whose eyes had opened for the first time in five days. She was looking at Ben as a beautiful smile tried to reach across her face.

Ben leaned in closer, his lips a soft caress on her cheek as she said, "I love you." Ben repeated the endearment. Virginia hadn't spoken a word in weeks. Comatose was the word she used when she reported each morning. Comatose. Jennifer heard the words, "I love you," weak and tired and in the whisper of Virginia's last breath.

Ben kissed his wife one last time. Jennifer turned away when she heard him say, "Goodbye."

And then...

the weight of waiting

Mary Carter

imperceptible to eyes
a palpable burden
settles the shoulders
pulls down the mouth
and finally closes eyes

the wait of weighing

Mary Carter

informed decisions
require some thought
while flights of fancy
rise like bubbles
soon gone with the wind

the way of weighting

Mary Carter

prioritize, all counsel says...
don't yield to the tyranny
of the urgent over the important
but sometimes the two converge
as in a diaper to be changed

How Long

June Rose Dowis

how long do you wait
in nature's abundance
before you finally see
the camouflaged gecko
who has you in his sight,
the snail making his way
slowly upon a gravel path
the persistent bumblebee
bending blossoms to earth
how long before the sun
seeps deep into your pores
thawing your very senses
until the fountain's rhythm
keeps time with your heart
how long 'til the birdsong
pierces your consciousness
and will you heed your soul
when these moments arrive,
and linger a moment more

Jim, my dearest friend,
with love,
Beth   *Dec. 2013*

Another Rollercoaster Ride

Beth Lynn Clegg

April 1, 1998. 10:35 p.m.

I picked up the receiver after silently cursing whoever had misdialed my phone number at this hour.

"Hello, Beth Lynn, this is Chastelain."

Those words sent shock waves of disbelief, followed by unspeakable joy surging through my body, threatening to take my legs from under me. It had been almost eight years since I'd heard from my eldest son. Emotions locked away by practiced diligence burst free in a torrent of words.

"Where are you? Let me come see you. I've prayed you'd call for so long, now all I can do is cry. I love you." These are things I recall saying.

His response was painfully revealing. "Sorry I missed you when you were in San Francisco eight years ago. I didn't get the message until after you'd left. Started to call four years ago then changed my mind. When I found a calling card on the street today I knew it was a sign I was supposed to call. I tried to reach both you and Patrick in Fort Worth and discovered you'd both moved back to Houston.

Leslie's number in Dallas is unlisted, so I called Uncle Frank and he gave me all three numbers. You'd be surprised what I find on the street. People are so careless. It's amazing."

We had prayed for this call; afraid to believe it would ever happen. Patrick had made two trips to California in an attempt to find his brother. His sister Leslie and I had both made one. So much had occurred since we lost contact with him. His father and grandmother Clegg had died. He had a niece and another nephew. That made four young people who needed to know their Uncle Ted, or Chastelain as he was now called after legally changing his name.

But, how much time was left on the card? I couldn't lose him. Not now. Not again. Oh, please, God, not again.

"Where are you?"

"A pay phone in San Mateo. Left San Francisco awhile back. Didn't listen when I was told not to go to the Tenderloins where thousands of people hang out. Got my head split open. I'm fine now. May even go back up there again sometime. I'm still living on the streets."

His words struck fear in my heart but his voice sounded strong. My next words continue to haunt me. "Thank God you're ok, Chastelain, but we can talk about it later. The card could expire at any moment. Give me the number and I'll call you back." It took three attempts for my trembling finger

not an absence of action; rather...it waits on the right time to act...in

to press the correct digits. A recorded message came on immediately and brought my world crumbling down around me.

California pay phones are blocked from incoming calls in an effort to curtail drug dealing.

I became hysterical. How long would he wait by a phone that was never going to ring? How could I live with the possibility that he might believe I had not intended to call back? I phoned Patrick, screaming my message of despair and disbelief into the receiver. He contacted Southwestern Bell. They refused to help. We could accomplish nothing from Houston. I felt God had abandoned me.

* * *

Eighteen hours later Patrick and I were in San Mateo. A phone company official provided the location of the pay phone in a matter of minutes and we were on the way. Someone would surely recognize the photo of Chastelain. Our expectations were unfounded. The service station attendant shook his head, but finally agreed to place the poster with Chastelain's picture and our contact information in the window. "There are so many," he said, unable to look us in the eyes. I walked to the side of the building and touched the phone – the instrument that had disconnected me from my son. I stared, prayed, willed Chastelain to be there, as he had been the night before. How could that be too much to ask?

Yet, fantasy was quickly replaced by reality as we contacted the police, hospitals, and homeless shelters. They took our information and posted his picture. He had no police record, had not been admitted to any county hospital, or signed in at any of the numerous shelters or soup kitchens in the area. We rode in silence, each lost in our own thoughts as we made our way along unfamiliar streets, looking intently at every man who fit Chastelain's physical description. I was afraid to speak for fear I might come unraveled.

We left sidewalks to follow earthen paths beaten down through dense foliage lining creeks. When Patrick disappeared into underbrush and did not return for several minutes I felt my heart would burst through my chest. My imagination was running wild as I prayed for his return. I'd lost one son. I couldn't survive losing them both. He reappeared after locating areas under a bridge where people had slept recently or sought shelter from the elements.

Our search seemed futile until we met three men coming out of a soup kitchen who claimed they'd seen him at a park close to the service station. We ignored the speed limit as we raced to the park, cursing red lights along the way, unable to keep our hopes from soaring to new heights. Homeless people were everywhere. He had to be here. We dashed into public restrooms. Patrick climbed over bleachers, stepping over sleeping men who never knew he was there. Circled maintenance buildings, looked through dense shrubbery. Spoke with everyone who would stop and listen or was sober enough to respond.

The policeman who recorded our information had warned Patrick and me to stay away from homeless people, as they might be dangerous. Yet, my son was one of these people he was referring to and we knew he could never be dangerous. It was unthinkable. We pressed on. We found a woman who said she'd worked with Chastelain cleaning downtown streets every Saturday morning, starting at two a.m. Every worker received five dollars in cash when they finished. Could we believe her? We hoped it was true. It helped to think he had earned money instead of gaining it by someone's misfortune.

Four days, numerous individuals, several cities, and countless walking and driving miles later, we boarded a plane for Houston, our hearts broken. Again. Our animated conversation on the flight to California, and Patrick's unbridled joy at the prospect of bringing his brother home, were replaced by crushing disappointment and a familiar knot in my stomach. Another rollercoaster ride was over. Chastelain had dematerialized back into the shadows of the fog-shrouded landscape.

There could never have been a crueler April Fool's joke.

* * *

is long, my dream of you does not end." Nuala O'Faolain ~§~ *"We*

Patrick made another trip to the area but the trail was cold and he was throwing good money after bad. He contacted Pinkerton Detective Agency and learned he'd done as much and more than they could do and saved himself $75.00 an hour. We had to acknowledge that unless Chastelain chose to contact us we would not hear from him again.

In order to finalize his father's and grandmother's estates held in limbo, we had Chastelain declared deceased. As Patrick said, "Mom, when we find him we'll have him declared undead."

Lasting Impressions

for Mom on Mother's Day

Carolyn T. Johnson

The nurse patted Mom on the arm
and said, "It won't be long now."
My lips felt parched.

Mom in a blue, gauze shower cap,
waiting patiently outside the operating room,
saw me apply lipstick and asked to borrow it.

I handed her my pale pink shade
and watched as she traced the
outline of her lips from memory,

lips that now looked identical to mine.
I offered a fresh tissue from my purse.
She blotted and gave it to me to discard,
but a little voice in my head said,
stop, fold it away, save it.

The anesthesiologist said, "It's time."
I bent down, kissed Mom's pale pink lips
and whispered in her ear,
"See you soon, Sunshine."

I felt my throat tighten, I had to look away.
I waved over my shoulder as I walked out
through the double doors.

After several hours in the waiting room,
anxious for news, I rifled my purse for a pen
and stumbled on the neatly folded tissue.

I let out a tiny gasp, put my fingertips to my lips
and lightly traced the outline, my mother's outline.

And knew it was time to mother my own mother,
I prayed that I got the chance.

In the Offing

Sarah Geil

I'll wait seven days, then throw away his toothbrush,
His smile still crested upon it.

Thirteen days, I'll remove his chair,
Still impressed with his body.

I'll wait thirty days to delete his Facebook.
His friends, 711, won't notice.

Sixty-two days, I'll box his clothes.
They'll no longer clutch his scent.

I've always been a planner.
Predictable as a calendar.
I didn't plan for this.

I'll wait to realize he will never return.
I'll wait until I can join him.

The Waiting Game
Kathe Campbell

It's been said that today is the tomorrow that you spent your time worrying about yesterday. Kind of crazy, but that was me recently.

Consumed with a bad case of jitters, I picked up the phone to make an appointment with my doctor, for I had found a good-size lump on my thigh. A lump, I pondered – just what I need. I've lost an arm, now I'm about to lose a leg. How wonderful, as I pictured myself a sorry, crippled old prune keeping my little ranch and stock in good fettle. Along with a new hip, rheumatoid arthritis and spinal stenosis, it was just one more thing to raise my walking drugstore status.

My doctor inspected the lump and advised sending me downstairs for blood work, then headlong into radiology under a gargantuan machine resembling some medieval torture device. "I really don't think it's anything to worry about, Kath," he remarked as I pulled on my jeans and began that awful waiting game.

Whether my doctor was worried about me or not, those were the words I wanted to hear. It was an expression of reassurance and comfort that allowed me to return to daily routines without anxious wondering about what lab reports would bring. When feeling uptight, I'll simply take deep breaths to avoid panic and sleepless nights. Whatever it is, it will no doubt be cured easily in these days of modern miracles – I kept telling myself.

Communication has always been important between me and my doctor. He puts me at ease, is relaxed, and treats me with courtesy and respect, even when I broach the silliest questions. Always well informed and actively involved in my own decision making and treatment, I consider his bedside manner the best. This terminology is interesting in that my doctor/neighbor contact rarely occurs bedside in the hospital, but in his office, or as we wave, out on our mountain road.

Unable to think much past my little anxieties, I pushed in a half-dozen CDs and plunged into a major kitchen and pantry makeover. Saving aside a box of items for the food bank and reorganizing drawers and cupboards made one afternoon fly. The next day I tackled the linen closet, and day three found me fine-tuning two bathrooms. Physical exercise and wearing myself to a frazzle left me gratified and did wonders for my disposition. Now if I should suddenly call it a day, my children could say..."Yes, our mom was such a meticulous homemaker!"

Four eternal days passed and fear commenced creeping in like hoarfrost, leaving me coldly bummed,

and characterized by episodes of chest pain, palpitations, shortness of breath and profuse sweating. There's no doubt about it, I was dying despite my doctor's reassurances, and I thought about calling his office to see what the holdup was. How long can it take for a lab crew to check out all those samples?

"We're headed up the mountain to spend the night, Gran," came cell phone voices from two beloved granddaughters who cared mightily about me in between college exams and jobs. It was all I could do to down pizza and sodas, but God love 'em, they were so comforting and funny. I crawled into bed less of a wreck, but in the middle of the night woke up wired, pacing about, my canine pal dogging my every step. Wooziness and nausea consumed me, and I had trouble reading the newspaper or absorbing TV. My imagination was on a rampage again, and if I wasn't sick before, I was doing a bang-up job giving myself a full-blown panic attack.

The following day I again bugged my sweet daughter with my woes and did my volunteer duty, and the dog and I took a little ride in the truck to drive out worry demons. But in the end, could the amazing truth be that the God of the whole world might be interested in little ol' me? It must have been so, for I knew somebody up there had His eye on this pitiful sparrow.

When I heard the doctor's nurse on the phone, I froze. Why was Maura calling, and not my doctor?

"The x-rays, ultrasounds, and lab results show nothing, Kath. Doctor says all is well. It's just a large noninvasive fatty lump. Watch it, and if it changes, be sure to come in, okay?"

How silly, I reflected, getting my tail all tied up in a dozen knots over this crazy thing. Well now, I certainly won't be doing that again, I joyously trumpeted aloud. All that stuff falling through the worry cracks in my life must be confetti, because waiting around for one's undoing is silly, and I feel like having a party.

Night Watch

Becky Haigler

> *In the fourth watch of the night Jesus went to them, walking on the sea. And when the disciples saw him, they were troubled, saying, "It is a spirit;" and they cried out for fear. But Jesus spoke to them saying, "Be of good cheer; it is I; be not afraid." Matthew 14:25-27*

It's that fourth watch that gets me, Lord,
that middle-of-the-night time
when nothing interrupts
my runaway mind. That's when
the account is overdrawn and the lump
turns into cancer; children run away

daughter, that which you wait for the longest you treasure the most,

to Timbuktu or to the circus.
And all I can do is watch. Which is better
than bleating about ghosts, but still
doesn't seem an act of faith. I want to *do*
something, fix something, but You
just want me to be: cheerful,
unafraid. And Your presence makes it
possible. I watch You walk on water
and believe I can do the same. Call me;
I will come out of fourth-watch despair
to walk with You – over open mouths
of piranha and alligator, dance
on hurricane waves and flood waters;
smile until day breaks.

Spring Rains Were Late That Year

SuzAnne C. Cole

Brassy sun wilts tender wheat yellow
shrivels corn into hollow husks as pigs
pant in dry wallow below the rattling windmill.
Worn out with waiting for the grace of rain
my German grandfather curses the blank sky.

Dancing Shoes

Tanya Bryan

In the morning I found
Two pairs of shoes
Sitting at the edge of my lawn
Looking like two people
Stepped out of them to dance
In the cool, midnight grass
But then never retrieved them.
The shoes waited
For their owners
All night
Next to the dewy sward,
Mouths gaping,
Tongues lolling
Waiting to be filled —
Warmed by their
Owners' feet.

We Are Waiting Still

Dixon Hearne

In 1968 – at the height of the Vietnam War – my brother Greg enlisted in the U.S. Marine Corps, just ahead of the draft. Like so many of my generation, I questioned our involvement in the affairs of a nation halfway 'round the globe. For one thing, Congress had never officially declared war, which technically made our presence "police action." Had we learned nothing from our police action in the Korean conflict? For another far more important thing, we were talking about the life of my dear brother. Daily newspapers and TV reportage brought only images of fear and despair to American households. But the real pain and heartache came with the long waits between letters home.

My mother, like so many others, dutifully prepared care packages at regular intervals – cookie tins, fudge, magazines, pictures – whatever was allowable. Nine tense months crept by, and although he was due for a leave in three more, I just couldn't wait. I packed a small suitcase, walked the three miles to Interstate 20 and thumbed my way across country to El Toro, California, where Greg was now stationed. Unannounced and disheveled, I presented myself at the Marine base. I explained to the two guards who I was and why I was there. Looking back, I can't help believing that pity alone gained me entrance onto the base.

Although my brother could not be immediately located, I was escorted to a Quonset hut where he had been assigned. Dead tired and hungry, I asked a couple of Marines where I might find a bite to eat while I waited for my brother. As it turned out, they had just arrived from the same tour of duty and knew Greg well. They fed me and settled me into his clean, crisp bed before they charged off on assignments. I felt a bit like Goldilocks, and, like her, I dozed soundly – belly full and content.

I awoke to the sensation of someone jostling my entire body. "What are you doing here?" my brother said, his face aglow with astonishment. "How did you get onto this base?"

"I hitchhiked," I proudly announced, "all the way from West Monroe."

We hugged for a long while, but I could tell he was concerned about my getting us both into trouble at the base. I explained how the guard escorted me to the barrack and how his buddies had fed me and showed me his sleeping quarters. Nonetheless, my visit was for one day only.

That evening I called the Kappa Sigma fraternity house at Long Beach State University, explained my situation, and within an hour two fraternity pledges were waiting for me at the guard shack.

Because it was summer, there were a couple of vacant beds at the fraternity house. I had once again fallen on good fortune. This meant that I could visit my brother and he could visit me every chance we got. In the meantime, my fraternity brothers were quite charitable – even showed me a great time and got me a job flipping patties at McDonald's.

Greg would catch a ride with buddies to see me every chance he got. In a loaned car, we rode up and down Pacific Coast Highway, even cruised into Hollywood and Santa Monica. We felt so young and alive and happy to be together again. But our visit was soon saddened by news from home that two boyhood friends had been killed in action. Shortly afterward, Greg received orders to report to Camp LeJeune – which deferred his leave indefinitely. I had managed to save enough money by this time for a return trip home by Greyhound bus, the longest trip I've ever taken. Worry set in again, and I couldn't help picturing my poor mother age another ten years overnight when Greg told her his leave was cancelled. She had waited so long to see her son safely returned to her, and now he would again be sent in harm's way. Some sinister form of double jeopardy, I felt sure.

My own return was bittersweet at best. Restlessness settled upon our home and remained there. I went through the motions of attending my classes at the local university, but my mind and heart were occupied with matters greater than an education – preparation for an uncertain future. Mother continued her regimen of carefully preparing and shipping care packages, writing daily letters – many of them crowded with newspaper clippings and snapshots. She never included obituary clippings about other fallen servicemen from our hometown.

And then it happened. On a summer-soft morning, one year from the date of his redeployment to Chu Lai, Greg magically appeared on our doorstep. I was too deep in sleep to hear the initial commotion, my mother's laughter and tears. Greg had wanted to surprise us, to capture us going about our daily lives. I was jarred back into existence by my brother's own hand, stirred from my dark dreams of war and waiting. In a heartbeat, we were whole again.

In the coming days I could feel the tension gradually exiting my body, my being. My mother's pleated brow and sunken eyes seemed amazingly rejuvenated, and the color of life returned to her face. Her sweet son, she now learned, would spend the remainder of his military duty safely on American soil. Like so many other families during that turbulent era, we had waited and prayed the precious hours and days for good news, for a world at peace. We are praying still.

Two Verses from the Waiting Room
Fern G. Z. Carr

I

Sitting in the reception area of the
Diagnostic Imaging Department,
I try to repress mental images
of a claustrophobic MRI machine
and its incessant jackhammering;
wasn't it only last year
that I was in this same place
waiting for him to have a CT Scan,
transfixed by the "Radiation Danger" sign
perched above heavy closed doors,
mesmerized by its red warning light
that blinked for the forty-five minutes
it took a radiology technician
to take x-rays of his brain —
Brain?
What brain?
You have a brain?
I used to tease;
apparently he does
and no one knows what is wrong with it.

II

At the hospital for yet another test –
diagnostics in an adjacent room,
the door is ajar and I catch a glimpse
of him lying on a narrow table with
electrodes taped to his scalp;
I strain to hear the technician's words,
anxious to snatch stray bits of information
but conversation is muffled by
a boom box whose music assaults
my left ear and forces
the right to do my bidding.
I want and don't want to be here;
I want to write a poem while I wait —
desperate for the comfort of my own words
but not having any paper on which to write them.
I catch glimpses of institutional-sized
laundry carts as they periodically lumber by
and I listen to spy codes over the intercom
as doctors are politely paged
to rush to the aid of the dying.

Machine No. 5 or, The Secret Life of Laundry

John Vicary

"Jing-Wei! Where are you? *Ai!* I need you!"

Jing-Wei lets her head fall back against the concrete wall. She is hiding, wedged behind empty laundry carts and unpacked boxes of detergent, but her mother's strident tone carries all the way into the back room, and ignoring it will do her no good. Jing-Wei knows from experience that the longer she takes to find out what her mother wants, the worse it will be in the end. Jing-Wei turns down the corner of her page in a dog-ear and closes the book. Perhaps she'll have time to finish the chapter if she fixes the problem as quickly as possible.

"*Ai ai ai!* Jing-Wei, faithless daughter!"

Jing-Wei winces. This is one of the times she is glad that her mother speaks only Chinese; at least no one can understand what she is saying. "I'm here, Mama." She steps out into the front of the laundromat, blinking in the glare of the bright lights after the comfort of being cocooned in relative darkness. Jing-Wei has always preferred the solitude of stolen moments to the hustle of the front of the shop.

"Number five isn't working again, and something is making noise in number two. Also, twelve is abandoned. Again." Her mother gestures towards the dryer in the corner that seems to break down the most. "I called Mr. Han, but he is too busy to come until the morning. Pshaw! May shame find him, that he doesn't make time for his own neighbors. You can look at it. You have gotten good at fixing them the last few times, and I have to go over the ledgers."

"Fine, Mama." Jing-Wei sighs and goes over to the errant dryer in a show of submission, but the truth is she doesn't mind fiddling around with the machines. Out of all the responsibilities she has running the family laundromat, fixing the washers and dryers is probably her favorite. Not because she is inclined towards engineering, but because it is usually something easy to figure out. Jing-Wei isn't foolish enough to tell Mama that, and if she looks at the machines and can't fix them, there is always Mr. Han as a backup. It gives her time away from mopping floors, lifting crates and translating customer complaints: the drudgery which makes her days endless and her future bleak.

Jing-Wei approaches dryer number five, their most unreliable machine. Her mother thinks it is cursed, but Jing-Wei has a different theory. The first few times it broke down, she had to take out the connecting hose, and she found a pair of sun-glasses stuck in the vent. One time, the lint trap was clogged with what looked to be an entire box of shredded tissues. On a fairly regular basis, Jing-Wei has been called to fix minor problems with the same dryer or the adjacent washer, and they all have issues with things getting stuck in the plumbing of the machines.

Jing-Wei was irritated at first. It was clearly the same patron who couldn't be bothered to check his or her pockets. The day would come when he would leave something that would permanently damage the laundromat, and Mama didn't charge enough to cover the overhead of a recklessly damaged machine.

One day, though, she began to take stock of the items: an army soldier. A packet of Lapsang Souchong tea (it didn't survive the rinse cycle). A box of nails. A CD labeled in Sharpie "Grand Funk Railroad" (it didn't survive the timed-dry setting). There was a deck of tarot cards and once, a slim vial of perfume. At Halloween, a little pumpkin was left on the very corner of machine number five, perched as if in offering.

Jing-Wei never saw the same person around; there was never a note of explanation. No one claimed the items, and there didn't seem to be any coherence to them. And yet, as the weeks wore on, she began to have the feeling that they were left deliberately. For exactly what reason, she couldn't say. She didn't want to admit it, but the idea intrigued her, and she almost looked forward to the dryer jamming. At least it was something interesting to break up the monotony of her days.

Then the notes started arriving.

Machine number five would stop working, and when Jing-Wei examined it, she wouldn't find an item, but a scrap of paper with a random verse. She hadn't studied poetry enough to know what the meaning was – or if it was written by the person leaving the notes or by someone else – but it was always beautiful.

When Jing-Wei gets to the dryer, she can see that it is empty. When she tries the handle, though, she can feel something taped to it. Jing-Wei cranes her neck around, and sees the note. Against her will, her heart flutters. She pries off the tape with a fingernail and unfolds it. *What will it say? Will it explain what is going on?*

The paper is unlined, and in the very center, written in careful script, it says:

> *Your ghost will walk, you lover of trees,*
> *(If our loves remain)*
> *In an English lane*

Jing-Wei frowns. What's this? It isn't meant for her, it seems, as she has no idea what to make of it. She is no one's lover, and isn't sophisticated enough to begin to guess at the writer's intent, other than it has been left for someone else all along. She cocks her head and re-reads the verses. They are graceful, beckoning, as if someone is trying to collude with her to be a part of something she doesn't understand, and she is running to keep from being left behind. She is ashamed, as if she's been spying into the windows of a stranger's home. This – whatever this is – isn't hers.

Disappointment is a cold stone in Jing-Wing's breast. She has never realized how much she has come to look forward to this. Is her life this lacking that she should peer into the lives of others for relief? The truth of it is a bitter pill to swallow, and Jing-Wei knows she should return the note. It isn't for her, and it has no meaning she can decipher. Yet her eyes drink in the words, and she yearns to be seduced. If only someone wanted her that way, enough to take her from the steam and press and toil of this place. If only someone would ask her so elegantly and in such a way – Jing-Wei wants to be free of this place, with her nagging mother and the constant whine and clang of machines. These washers are her salvation and her damnation, all wrapped up in the form of hard work and inheritance, monetary and filial duty.

Jing-Wei swallows down the taste of detergent; the powder seems to have permeated her skin and coated her tongue. She can't even breathe without perceiving the fumes of this place in her very lungs. She imagines that she is made of nothing but soap, that one day she might blow away, light as a bubble

of my heart, and never forget, that until the day God will deign to re-

on the breeze, or turn to foam and rinse down the drain without leaving a trace. When she was a child, she remembered a story from her childhood about a girl who turned to seafoam as a sacrifice, and at the time it seemed a terrible reprimand that her young mind could hardly bear. Now it doesn't seem so bad a fate. How curious that the intervening years make punishment appear as escape.

She smooths her hands over the creases in the paper, feeling the words intended for some lucky girl. This cryptic message – maybe it is merely a half-finished cheat-sheet for a test? Jing-Wei should throw it away.

And yet she slips it into the pocket of her jeans as she goes to see about the thumping in number two, which turns out to be nothing more than an unbalanced load.

* * *

"Jing-Wei!"

"Mama."

"I need your help. Number five is not working! Didn't you fix it on Thursday? It must have a bad spirit! I will call Mrs. Yi from next door. Maybe she can do a ceremony to lift the curse."

"No, Mama. Just let me look at it again." Jing-Wei checks the calendar. Mama is right. She fixed it last Thursday. Whoever comes is getting more regular; this makes three Thursdays in a row now. Jing-Wei tries not to get excited. "I think I know what the problem is."

"Lazy girl!" Mama throws her hands up in the air and walks away.

Jing-Wei almost skips to the machine. She checks behind the handle, but there isn't a note. Undaunted, she opens the door, but it is empty. The lint tray is dust-free and clear of debris. Her heart falls a little. Still, Mama said it wasn't working, so something must be wrong. Jing-Wei reaches behind, but there is nothing.

Her eyes fall on the coin slot, into which something is jammed. The jolt of excitement makes her fingers shake, and she slides the note out with care. It is folded the same way, and this week she recognizes the writing. The words, however, are just as cryptic:

Yet knowing how way leads on to way,
I doubted if I should ever come back.
I shall be telling this with a sigh
Somewhere ages and ages hence.

In the corner is a pencil sketch of her face. It was done with amazing skill, and Jing-Wei trembles as she looks at the image of herself. It is just a little thumbnail drawing – it must not have taken very long – but she has this lonely expression in her eyes; she is gazing out and wondering what lies beyond the plate-glass windows of this trap that is her destiny. She thought that longing was hidden, that she kept it locked away deep in her breast, but whoever caught her unaware has seen past that. Who is he? What does it mean?

Jing-Wei jerks her head up, hoping to catch someone's reaction as he watches her read the note, but there is no one in the laundromat. She is alone.

As she turns the scrap of paper over, she notices a detail that she missed the first time around. It is addressed to "Small Bird." Someone knows her well enough to know what her Chinese name means. She chews her lip as her confusion grows and the lines swirl from the poem. *I doubted if I should ever come back...with a sigh...ages and ages...somewhere ...*

This is the last note, she realizes. There will be no more.

"Jing-Wei, have you done your job? Is every-thing fixed now?" Mama shouts as the evening rush fills the laundromat.

Jing-Wei blinks away the tears that have gathered, unnoticed, under the lids of her eyes. For a brief moment she dared dream of more, but now she can see clearly again. "Yes, Mama. Everything is as it should be," she calls.

"Do as you wish! Such a lazy girl. Help me with this register! My feet hurt tonight, and I need some-one to keep watch on it while I sit and have a cup of tea." Mama rubs her back. "I'm ready for a break, but you can keep going for a while, huh?"

"Yes, Mama," Jing-Wei nods and puts the paper in her pocket. She will be sure to save this little scrap of hope; unlike her careless admirer, she will

Forgetting is painful. But not knowing which to do is the worst kind

see to it that this will not bleed out through any wash cycles. Jing-Wei steadies herself and turns to face her mother. "I'll be here as long as you need me."

We Wait for You

Claudia Mundell

You, little fellow, are holding our hearts
Long before you can lace twiggy fingers
Around our tree-stump thumbs.
We have seen you floating in your sea cave
Budding, developing, growing, becoming.
Now we learn there is a shadow that hides
In the folded wrinkles of your brain,
Upsetting the once-perfect picture.
Yet, this fearful knot of unknowing matter
Is part of you, and we wait to see
What this silhouette means.
We wait with you;
We wait for you —
For all of what you bring.

Slow Cooking

Renee Emerson

The sumac limbs sag,
the vow of winter already
weighing.

A late dinner, drowsy, shaping bread
on the baking stone.

Yellow squash, onions, carrots,
a roast and small potatoes
slow-cooking.

My hands bitter with onions,
apron on, the long soak of waiting
for you to come home.

My self-reliance, old trophy,
what once carried me,

swallowed
in the night's cataract, the moon,

and stars like small umbrellas,
opening.

War, Worry, Wonder, Wait

Lois Kaskel Welch

War, worry, wonder, and wait. I hate it all. The only W that I want to see in big letters is in *Welcome home* – for Joe, Gene and Paul. The war in Europe has been over since early May. It is now mid-September and still my husband and two of my brothers have not returned to our little Ohio town. We have heard that a shortage of ships to transfer all the military personnel back to the U.S. is causing the delay. A legitimate reason – but it doesn't relieve my frustration. I hate this waiting.

* * *

What a difference a day makes! Today Mom received a letter from my brother Gene. He says he may be leaving England near the 20th of this month on the Queen Mary, which would have him arriving in New York at the end of the month. His letter continues, "If I don't make it now, it could be weeks before the next ship. I'll call when I land in New York."

As we are finishing dinner the next night, Mom claps her hands to get our attention. "I have something to tell you. After spending last night worrying about it, I spoke to my supervisor this morning. Friday will be my last day at work."

We are all surprised and excited by her news. My youngest brother Dick asks, "Mom, are you gonna cook every day for us again?" Looking at me, he adds quickly, "Well, you can't cook like Mom does!"

He's right. I did my best, filling in for Mom, but I will be glad to turn control of the kitchen back to her.

Mom smiles. "You have all been so good at taking over the chores so I could take that job. You'll never know how much that means to me. But I need to be home when my boys arrive."

I know that Mom has enjoyed her time working outside the home and I wonder how much my older brother Paul's threat influenced her decision to quit. Since our dad died ten years ago, Paul has tried to step up to being the man of the house. When he first learned that Mom had taken a job, he was angry and upset. In a recent letter, he wrote, "No mother of mine should have to work. When I get home, I'll get you fired if that's what it takes to keep you at home."

I think Mom enjoyed being part of the work force during the war. But having her boys back home will keep her plenty busy. She will cater to their every wish. And she will love it.

* * *

It's the last day of September. Mom and I have been housecleaning for a week. Today we have risen early and are well into our baking schedule when my seven-month-old daughter Joyce wakes up – hungry. She fusses as I give her a bath and dress her in clean clothes, but calms down when I put her in her high chair. When she's fed, I place her chair near where we are working in the kitchen. She's happy to watch us and play with a toy on her tray. Before long, she will be meeting her uncle Gene. And, pray God, it won't be too much longer before her daddy comes home to see her for the first time.

I look at Mom and say, "You know, it's the end of the month."

She frowns at me, "Don't say it! He will call today. I'm certain!"

I wish I could be so sure. We work in silence for a while.

Then Mom says, "I'm sorry I spoke sharply. But I have to believe he will call. It's all I have left." There are tears in her eyes.

Patting her arm, I tell her, "It's all right. The waiting is getting to all of us."

It takes most of the day, but we finish baking in time to get dinner on the table. As we wait for my sisters Kack and Cille and my brother Dick to get home from their jobs, Mom takes Joyce in her arms and heads for the rocking chair. "You sat in that high chair too long today. You and I are going to take a nap."

Mom's rocking chair creaks its comforting rhythm and I have just sat down when the phone rings.

Mom hands Joyce to me and hurries to answer. "Hello? Gene! I knew it was you. Where are you?"

Mom angles the phone's receiver toward me and I huddle close to hear his voice. Gene is laughing, "Mom, I'm in New York. I'll be in Lima tomorrow at 3:30. It's great hearing your voice. I haven't talked to you in three years and you sound just the same!"

"Oh, Gene, I'm so glad you're on your way home."

"I love you, Mom. All I want to do is get home, get a hot shower and into some civilian clothes. I have to hang up now – hundreds of guys are waiting to call home. See you tomorrow!"

* * *

Too nervous to sleep, Mom and I are both up early next morning. After eating breakfast, Mom peels potatoes for tonight's supper. Then she gets out her best tablecloth and napkins, her best dishes and the good silverware. She bustles from one task to another, unable to sit still for a minute.

By mid-morning she has everything prepared and it's clear she needs something to keep her busy.

"Get ready, Mom. We're going uptown to buy some new clothes for Gene."

Mom offers no argument and within a half-hour I have Joyce and myself ready. In no time at all, we

who Grieve, / Too Short for those who Rejoice; / But for those who

find grey slacks, a white shirt, and a neat blue pullover. I'm hoping Gene hasn't changed sizes since he's been gone.

By 2:30 p.m., Mom and I have packed up Joyce and are heading for Lima. Arriving at the train station a half-hour later, we find a parking spot close by the entrance. My sister Pauline has walked over from her apartment with little Paul in his stroller. Mom leads and Pauline and I follow her into the station.

We find seats and check the board. New York Arrivals: ON TIME. We have a while to wait and we try to talk, but we are so anxious, we find ourselves repeating the same phrases: "What time is it now?" "Did you hear that? I think it's a train whistle." "I hope he gets here soon." "What time is it now?"

Eventually we hear the train coming. Hurrying outside, we watch it come to a stop. The doors open and, right away, we see Gene step onto the platform. He is walking toward us and, seeing Mom, he hurries to meet her, drops his luggage, and gathers her up in his arms.

Gene manages to keep his arm around Mom as he picks up his suitcase. They make their way through the crowd to where Pauline and I stand. With hugs and tears, we greet our brother, and introduce our babies to him. He is overwhelmed. Taking each one in his arms, he holds them, saying, "I'm going to have to get acquainted with you two!"

Love, / Time is not." Henry van Dyke ~ § ~ "You can't stay in your

We are met by Pauline's husband Scoot, as he's coming from work to pick them up. They head to their car to follow us home. Mom tosses the keys to Gene, saying, "I hope you remember how to drive this car!"

The ride back to Delphos is a blur of laughter and pleasant chatter. Mom and I are delighted just to hear Gene's voice.

Kack, Cille and Dick are all home from their jobs and greet Gene excitedly.

"There's time for you to take that shower before dinner," Mom says.

I hand him the clothes I bought for him and he smiles. While Gene showers and puts on "civvies" for the first time in three years, we girls help get the food on the table. Mom has made Gene's favorites: baked pork chops and dressing, mashed potatoes with gravy, corn, and noodles.

Gene emerges in his new clothes and I am relieved to see they fit him well. When we are all seated, Mom leads us in the traditional Catholic prayer before meals: "Bless us, Oh Lord, and these Thy gifts which we are about to receive from Thy bounty, through Christ, Our Lord. Amen."

Gene praises Mom for the delicious meal and she teases him, "Well, since you're so appreciative, you might get dessert, too!"

Later she brings out butterscotch cookies and custard pie, Gene's favorite sweets. We take our time enjoying dessert and coffee and spend the

corner of the Forest waiting for others to come to you. You have to go

rest of the evening laughing, talking, and remembering old times together.

I'm so happy my brother is home. Yet, my happiness is incomplete. My husband Joe and my brother Paul are still in Europe – still waiting to come home. Soon, I hope.

Lines scribbled on a boarding pass
Laura Matheson

Heart one place, body another,
A full day's travel separates us.
I wonder: Will I get there in time?
My heart leaps, fueled by bad coffee.
It takes strength to sit, to wait
As my fragmented mind barely copes.
Time squelches, fractured, aimless,
As if mired in black prairie mud.
Hope gives my soul new sustenance.
I can only wait, until I arrive.

That Sound Only

Charles Leggett

The elevator opened and was empty.
No one stepped in or out. It quietly closed,
And of all sounds, I heard that sound only.

Someone inside had changed his mind; an early
Leave-taking, perhaps by some mistake, was
    caused.
The elevator opened and was empty

—No one here waited for it, certainly
Not I, standing in silence, bemused.
And of all sounds, I heard that sound only,

The silence of the corridor, of me,
Of flights of stairs, of ashtrays long disused.
The elevator opened and, though empty,

Wore surfaces akin to mirrors, shiny,
Opaque until around passengers enclosed.
And of all sounds, I heard that sound only

As it rumbled closed so quietly —
Its bell, in its own echoes soon suffused.
The elevator opened and was empty,
And of all sounds, I heard that sound only.

Raptors of the Deep

John A. McColley

I'm told I will be in this small metal room for the next five to six hours. They don't seem to understand the danger. I know what I saw. It was no hallucination. It wasn't the raptures of the deep as Dr. Simmons insists – it was the raptors! No one will listen, though. All I can do is record what I know I saw.

It began with a normal survey dive. I was taking readings and pictures of frilled sharks and other creatures at about seventy meters down. I couldn't believe what I saw, but I did see it and I got pictures. Those creatures, walking upright like men, but without dive suits or tanks. They were scaly, with powerful legs adorned by those great hooked claws, one per foot like in that movie. It was all I could do to keep from crying out, losing my mouthpiece.

The lizard men were carrying something between them as pall bearers at a funeral, with the object between them, three on the left and the right. They were walking when I first caught sight of them, but they came to a cliff and swam off as though the stone pillar they carried weighed nothing. Through

I'm going. So I don't have to wait until I die to start seeking a Great

the eyepiece of the camera, I saw carvings on the pillar. There, lizards and serpents cavorted. Strings of incomprehensible symbols created waves and swirls like currents.

I signaled to Fredericks and fled for the surface, forgoing the decompression protocols. I was sure, after the flashes of the camera, my panning head-lamp cutting through the Stygian gloom, that they had seen us. We needed to remove ourselves as quickly as we could. I called *The Cormorant*, telling them we were coming. Dr. Simmons told me to abide and rise by levels, but there was no time. I looked back for Fredericks, but he was gone. They'd gotten him.

* * *

I can feel my head clearing even as I write this second entry. I remember coming up into the moon pool, flopping onto the deck, screaming for the harpoon guns, depth charges. I recall being frightened to the core, but I couldn't tell you why. Everything before I saw the light coming down from the moon pool is a blur of panic and swimming upward. Reading through my earlier entry, I can see I must have suffered from nitrogen narcosis. I claimed to get pictures of the alleged creatures, but I don't know where the camera went. I can only hope I didn't drop it in my panic. Maybe one of the crew has it.

How many hours has it been? I must have smashed my dive watch on the edge of the pool or a bulkhead. The crystal is cracked and it's been ten fifteen for what must be two hours. I hope I didn't hurt anyone with my flailing. What was that? A noise, from outside the ship. It sounds like a scratching, maybe drilling, but that's absurd.

"Dr. Simmons? Betty?" I say into the intercom beside the door. I pull back from the grille to look through the eight-inch circle window in the door itself. Betty waves to me and smiles. She presses a button on the panel before her and looks at the screen showing my vital signs.

"You're looking a bit better, Stan. Your heart rate has settled down and looks strong."

"Does that mean I get a reprieve? I am feeling much better, I promise. Do I have to wait the whole six hours?"

"I'm afraid you have to stay in there, Stan. It's not that bad. I left you a pencil and paper to write or draw or whatever and a few magazines. You can read if you like, or do a crossword. Now, unless you have an emergency in there, I have to see if I can fix Fredericks' monitors. We've lost his signal and I can't figure out why."

Lost Fredericks' signal. They don't know why. I know why. No, that's crazy... Was that tapping? I lean into the bulkhead across from the door. I hear, "tap tap tap, scratch, tap tap, scratch," as though claws are striking the surface and sliding along, trying to find purchase. I sit up away from the bulkhead and close my eyes, breathing through my nose to relax. I ignore the sounds. Obviously I'm still muddled from the raptures. I open my eyes and stand, picking up the crossword magazine. I sit on the little cot and open to the first puzzle.

* * *

At first, I ignore the banging, far louder than the tapping before, resounding in the small space where I'm trapped. I give up on the puzzle. Suspicion growing again that I may not have hallucinated all of what I saw below, I write down the events of the last couple of hours. I can tell time is passing by the clock set into the opposite bulkhead above Dr. Simmons' readouts. I'm half-way through my sentence. I wish I'd spotted it earlier. She works away, apparently oblivious to the terrible sounds echoing in the chamber. What can that mean but that I'm still imagining them? How could she not hear if they were real? The answer is obvious: the chamber is basically soundproof. That's why we need the intercom. Whatever's banging, it must be right outside the chamber on the side opposite Betty's station.

I'll record my experiences, describe the sounds, my suspicions. If it's real, someone should know if they ever find this journal. If it's not, then they can use it to track my madness as it progresses.

I lie in the cot for a while, hoping that sleep will come and usher me to health as my body returns to normal in the fleeting time of slumber. Instead, as I lie there, I hear the burbling language of the lizard

roll around it, let it slide like coins through you fingers. So much time

men as they communicate their plans to take *The Cormorant*. I toss, I turn, I hold the pillow over my ears, but still I hear them, faint, distant, malevolent. The final straw comes when a great shrieking of metal arises as though the ship is being rent in twain, forcing me to sit up and go to the chamber door. I look out, but see only Dr. Simmons' clipboard on the deck, pen rolling away, then back toward it as the ship shifts in the other direction.

I grab hold of the door frame, but the list is too violent and I lose my grip, falling and striking my head. I'm bleeding a little now, but it's not bad. Blood covers my hand, but head wounds always bleed excessively, even minor ones. My attempt to stand fails. The cold steel bulkhead slams into my back, my head. Darkness falls even as I hear static from above. Someone's trying to use the intercom. I fight for consciousness as the fluid voices ululate like water pouring from a full bottle. Glug, burble, glug. I hear my name in the confusion of sounds. Panicked, I huddle into the corner, remaining silent. A shadow passes before the window in the door. I hold my breath. The world goes gray.

* * *

Consciousness returns. Head pounding, I stagger to my feet, leaning heavily on the wall. Blood smears on gray painted steel as my hand slips. At the door, I push the call button on the intercom, but see no one in the next room. Computer screens sit blank. The lights flicker overhead. I lean to one side of the door, then the other, trying to see farther to the sides. No white-coated doctors, no blue-suited divers chat or look over charts. To some relief, there are no raptors, either. I don't hear their gurgling, or any banging.

Vainly, hopelessly, I pound on the thick steel door with the side of my fist. This hurts, so I pick up the small table where the magazines lie and fold it up. Swinging this with all my might, I manage to splinter the wood, sending pieces everywhere, but when I look out, there's no one. They've been taken.

My blood chills as I see movement outside the chamber. It's not Dr. Simmons in some dreadful state, neither is it a dagger-toed lizard man. It's simply water. A trickle turns into a stream as I watch. The clipboard surfs across the room, ramming ineffectually at the bulkhead below the hatch on the left. Nodding to myself, I know there's nothing left to do except set the table back up as well as it will stand on three legs and the front edge missing. I gather up the journal I had been filling out and record all that has happened from where I'd left off.

There's nothing else to do but write and wait. Or maybe I'll try to get in one more crossword.

wait for some other person, or if we wait for some other time. We are

The Simple Truth

B.J. Yudelson

I'm sitting in the back of the funeral chapel. The air conditioning barely beats the July heat. My mind drifts from the eulogy to a winter day 25 years ago. That day I sat up front. That day I shivered with grief and disbelief.

I remember watching an endless line of stricken faces file past to murmur comforting words – words I was beyond hearing. What could anyone say? What words could undo the work of the drunk driver?

I remember a rabbi telling me that because this was Purim Katan, a month before Purim in a Jewish leap year, eulogies were inappropriate. He and the other speakers would not extol Ruth, just speak the simple truth about her full, short life.

I remember Rabbi Jablon, with his red beard and kind eyes, telling the overflowing crowd how responsible Ruth was, how caring and giving, loved by all the children in the junior congregation she led at his synagogue. She was their role model, he said, mature beyond her thirteen years. Not a eulogy, just the simple truth.

Rabbi Kamen's usually twinkling eyes were sorrowful. Voice breaking, he described Ruth's kindness, her intelligence, and especially her love of children. Ruth babysat for his six children and tutored one of his daughters.

"Six children – how do you take care of six children?" I used to ask Ruth.

"Oh, this one had a friend over, that one was at a friend's house, another was napping, and that only left three to deal with," she would reply with an assurance that I, her mother, couldn't comprehend.

Tears ran in an unending stream down my face while other bearded men in dark suits praised Ruth's character and devotion to Jewish learning.

Outside the chapel I saw my younger daughter Miriam's best friend, Fagie, her dark hair and glasses a reminder of Ruth's Semitic beauty. Her familiar face was somber, her dimple gone. She seemed weighed down by her backpack, filled, I thought, with the shock of a young death. Later, I trembled under the February sky that pressed down on the cemetery. My father and I held each other up as we watched the coffin lowered.

We waited endlessly, painfully, interminably while people from Ruth's life threw dirt into the grave with the backs of their shovels, a traditional sign of reluctance to say good-bye. Her father. Her brother. Her Uncle Harry. Her cousin Peggy. Her friend Joey. Grim-faced teachers, crying friends. One put down the spade, and the next took it up.

Shovelful by shovelful, thud by thud, each clod crushed me with its finality.

My father, a Reform Jew, had never witnessed a burial at which the mourners filled in the grave. I remember his words. "This really clops you on the head. It doesn't let you deny that she is gone."

All I do is wait, I recall thinking. A lifetime of waiting in the thirteen days since the intoxicated driver's car had destroyed Ruth's brain stem and left my effervescent daughter comatose. And now more waiting while the hole in the ground slowly fills. Will it never end? How will I fill my emptiness? How will I keep going?

* * *

These jagged images, evoked by a neighbor's funeral, accompany me to a wedding my husband and I attend later in the day. The bride's sister, Rachel, was a classmate of Ruth; the wedding is in her garden. Under the healing sun, surrounded by happiness, my thoughts soften to visions of Ruth and Rachel at play, gossiping and giggling. My tears are gentle, shed in part for the bride's happiness, in part for all that will never be.

That night, we attend a fiftieth anniversary celebration for friends. With moist eyes, I picture four-year-old Ruthie at her grandparents' fiftieth anniversary. I recall how she smiled shyly at relatives she hardly knew, tagged along with cousins, and grimaced at the camera for the formal family portrait.

I prefer these memories, and others summoned by life, to the ones that assaulted me at the funeral. A grandchild's tantrum brings back Ruth's toddler fits – and my relief when she outgrew them. I catch sight of a sailboat, and suddenly Ruth is at the helm, jibing skillfully, thrilling to the wind in her hair. On a crisp January day, I can almost hear her singing along the snowy path from school, jacket unzipped to the frigid sun.

Like the hugs I long for, these memories caress me with a closeness to my eternally young middle child, whose eyes sometimes glimmer from the faces of her siblings' children. I look at these grandchildren, two named for their Aunt Ruth, and pray they will grow to adulthood.

* * *

Not long after Ruth's death, I sat with Rabbi Jablon in the synagogue library. "I wanted to know how she'd turn out," I wailed.

It has taken years to understand the simple truth of his answer.

"She turned out beautifully."

Gethsemane

Carol McAdoo Rehme

I feel abandoned, burdened, weak.
Is this my Gethsemane, Father?
I rubbed at the small of my back and gazed out the barred window of the waiting room to the deepening dusk outside. Headlights flickered as cars filed from the parking lot like fireflies in formation.

I felt as bleak and gray and cold as the darkening night.

A sigh shoved a path from my knotted stomach to my throat. It snagged on the jagged lump lodged there and erupted in a jerky whimper.

How long had I been at my own personal "midnight watch"? Hours. No, days. Did it even matter anymore?

A single phone call had disrupted our lives, altered our course. Perhaps forever.

At times throughout the day I had managed to hold Kyle, but never my own tears. Even now, they slipped down my cheeks, a mirrored reflection of the persistent rain pelting the glass windowpanes in front of me.

It had been a long day – bedside – in the Trauma Unit. After thrilling everyone with his initial, but sporadic moments of awareness earlier in the week, Kyle – victim of a hit-and-run drunk driver – now lapsed into unresponsiveness.

Absolute. Total. Complete.

Instead, a wild, aggressive agitation replaced his once-promising breaths of lucidity. I felt cheated somehow, like a child promised a coveted gift only to have it snatched away.

How dare You let my hope grow and then trample it like this?

For eleven hours that day, I had hovered over Kyle. Suctioning paste-thick mucus from dangerously full lungs. Encouraging him futilely while deep, painful coughs wracked his weakened body. Sponging his brow over and over and over again only to watch sweat beads pop out like measles. Quieting his flailing arms and legs that tangled the bedding and threatened the life-gifting tubes.

Wasn't it enough to deal with the combined traumas of blood clots, brain hemorrhages, broken bones, high fevers, and pneumonias? His problems read like a medical book index. Now, still comatose, Kyle was a danger to himself. Already his persistent thrashing had disturbed an IV and dislodged a catheter.

Someone ordered restraints. For Kyle's "own safety."

I stood by helplessly, waiting while a nurse – armed with two white corded belts – encircled my son's ankles and fettered him to the computer board at the foot of the bed. She shoved the fingers of each hand into mounded mitts, as plump as boxing gloves, which she manacled to the side rails.

There he lay, my twenty-one-year-old manchild. Constrained by shackles. Tethered by tubing. Strapped to his bed. And still he twisted and writhed.

He's my son, God, a human being! He isn't an animal. Must he be harnessed like one?

The unsaid words shoved roughly against my thoughts. I bit the inside of my cheek and swallowed the rusty taste of blood.

Each glance into the cement faces of the nurses and doctors screamed out reality. I knew I was standing at the lip of death's yawning chasm. Death – cold, clammy, and chilling. I sensed it; I smelled it; I shivered with it.

I fled Kyle's room and raced down the long hall.

Now I staggered under the burden that bowed my shoulders. The pain and uncertainty of a death-watch. Icy and dark, like the night shadows prowling the empty waiting room.

I am exhausted and as weary as the watchers at the tomb, Heavenly Father.

How much more can You ask of me?

~ *"We must be willing to let go of the life we planned so as to have the*

Death scenes, detailed and descriptive, flashed in erratic sequencing behind my eyelids. I massaged my temples to erase the grisly images that thrummed through my mind. My stomach quivered and clenched in protest against the weighted anguish that plummeted from my heart to settle there. Pressing my tear-stained cheek against the fogged window, I prayed.

I prayed for enough faith to bear this trial.

I prayed for enough faith to see it through.

I prayed for enough faith to believe that my son would live.

For enough faith to...

Oh, Father, this is too hard to manage, too heavy to carry, too much to ask of any mother. Please let this cup pass from me!

Please.

I prayed for the only thing I needed. Faith enough.

The Unending Wait

Sheryl L. Nelms

handmade quilt spread
in the green shade
of pecan tree

I wait for him

a cooler full
of strawberries
ready for his lips
and white teeth

to nibble

cream-dipped
and sugared

from my fingertips

I am patient
as the hour
comes for
him

to be here

but he isn't
so I sit

vowing never to leave
because then I
will be

stood up

A Rustling, Falling Leaf
Elizabeth Schultz

Leaves teach us how to die. ~ H. D. Thoreau

You wait for a friend to come,
a friend to go, a child to grow.
You wait for the car at the shop,
the car to stop, the report, the call,
the dentist's hygienist, your brother
to be released from surgery.
You wait for the waitress, for the bus.
You wait for sleep, for tomorrow.
You wait for something or nothing,
for nothing to become something,
for something to become nothing.
And when something or nothing
comes and leaves, when waiting
in the dim corridor is over,
you hear a rustling, falling leaf.

Stop at 3:11

Anthony J. Mohr

In April 1963, Miss Haberman, my sophomore English teacher at Beverly Hills High School, told us to write a paragraph starting with one of three topic sentences. I picked, "To me, most of my sister's girlfriends seem crazy," and for the next half hour, I delighted in saying why. "Hillary is a flirt whose lifetime goal is to kiss President Kennedy. Sharon's feet stink. I don't think she ever washes them." Several barbs later, I concluded as follows: "Finally, there is Lynne. She wrote me a letter saying, *I'll give you a big hug and kiss when you get back from camp.*"

I finished after three o'clock, moments before Lucie did. I wished she'd written me the letter Lynne had. Lucie sat two rows to my left and three seats closer to the front of the room, which made it hard to catch her attention. I wanted her to sense me gazing her way, but she didn't. She faced forward toward Miss Haberman, who was ostensibly grading our homework from Warriner's *English Grammar and Composition*, but probably was reading a Harlequin romance. With her thick glasses and her red hair in a bun, I assumed Miss Haberman yearned for a Prince Charming.

I stared at the wall clock and was sure it needed servicing. The minute hand would retreat half a notch before surging forward. And since this was late afternoon, the minute hand lingered too long over 3:10, as if time itself were taking its time.

I waited forever for 3:12, the magic minute that ended the school day. I waited so long, I forgot the fun I'd had trashing my sister's girlfriends. The boy to my right yawned, loudly enough to make Miss Haberman look up, but Lucie didn't turn. All I could see was a quarter of her face and the back of her lovely arm. I tried isometrics; I pushed against the back of my chair and put my palms against the edge of the desk – they were attached as a unit – and felt the metal struts give a little. Still, she didn't look.

3:11. The scratch of pens gave way to the rustle of papers as the class passed their assignments forward and closed their three-ring binders. A shoe scraped the floor. Someone whispered to me, and I suppressed a snort of a laugh.

My 1962 yearbook contained a photograph labeled "Parking lot... 3:11." Falcons and Tempests and Mercurys and Thunderbirds were bunched together between the school buildings and the back lot of Twentieth Century Fox, which bordered our campus. No one had photographed the faculty parking lot, where the cars were not nearly as new or sparkling.

The minute hand executed its backward feint to 3:10 before clicking forward to 3:12 and the blessed final bell.

Lucie got away before I could reach her, vanished into the parking lot, now vibrant with the gun of engines and the shouts of boys and girls who thought they were free. I wasn't yet. I had to wait three more weeks to take my driving test, which I'd fail, and then I'd have to wait for June to try again.

3:12 divided the day. To the right of those digits was adventure with Lucie, if I'd ever ask her out, which I had yet to do. I'd wait for tomorrow, or next week, for there would always be a 3:12. Or so I thought. I should have counted the 3:12s I had left.

But I didn't do the math, and on Friday night, as always, Ralph and Brad showed up unannounced. They came because they were adrift and liked to tie up at my house while they waited for their lives to start. Ralph stumble-jumped, mouth open, through the door, and Brad trailed behind, a smile on his rubber face. And because I didn't have the heart to shoo them off and do something constructive for a change, and because Ralph had just obtained his driver's license, I agreed to ride with them up to Hollywood, where he could show off his green Pontiac with – he said – a 400-cubic-inch V8 engine.

"You don't have a date tonight," Brad said, the master of the obvious. He puffed on his Marlboro.

I said no and rolled down the window. I couldn't stand smoke.

Ralph took a drag on his cigarette and gave me a smirk as he crawled through traffic on the Sunset Strip.

"Tony's a loooooser," he said.

* * *

I was too teenage-stupid to feel a tock when the clock ticked to 3:12. I was too dense to savor the run-up to that moment. How was I supposed to know that soon the days would take wing? They started to on June 14, when Larry, Jack, and I lowered the flag at the end of the Class of 1963's graduation ceremony. The service club to which we belonged, the Squires, traditionally had that duty.

To our right were the graduates, seated on the three tiers of the school's front lawn, looking out at the Hollywood Hills. Below them, on the grass, sat their families, who had to look up to see their children and the school's long, two-story building behind them.

The thought took form while a girl played a movement from Mozart's *Flute Concerto Number 2*, but I said nothing yet.

We lowered and folded the flag. Calmly, his voice already deep, Larry said, "Squires, left face," and because I took our job seriously, I turned square on my heels and marched with my friends to

you want to do is curl back up in that moment before things changed."

the school's main entrance, through the double doors and into the office, where we handed over the flag and turned into juniors.

That's when I articulated my thought. I said that half our high school careers were over.

"It scares me," Jack said.

* * *

The way Jack delivered those three words has never left me. Although his voice wobbled and sounded too loud, Jack had articulated exactly how I felt. It was as if I'd been issued an oversize blazer as a freshman, and now, two years later, I had not only grown into it, but through it, slowly tearing the seams. Worse, they kept ripping, for suddenly it was September 1963, and I was in Mr. Quinlan's English class, again my last class of the day.

The course theme, Mr. Quinlan said in his brilliant style, would be the nature of man. Projected on a screen was a picture of an athlete in need of a shave. "Here we see a virile young man, perspiring as all virile young men should, smoking a cigarette. What does this tell us about the nature of man?" He turned on a reel-to-reel tape recorder, and a news broadcast filled the classroom. "A spectacular crash on the Santa Ana Freeway killed two..."

"And what does that tell us about his audience?" Mr. Quinlan asked. "The announcer doesn't lead with Berlin or the space program. It's more important that someone died on the freeway..."

I didn't see the minute hand drop to 3:11, nor did I hear the click. The classroom overlooked the parking lot, but I didn't gaze out the window. Mr. Quinlan was listing the modern European plays we'd read in the coming weeks: *Tiger at the Gates, The House of Bernarda Alba, Mother Courage, Rhinoceros...*

This is what I should have thought: Stop at 3:11. Let me wait there, bunched together with my friends while Mr. Quinlan drives question after question toward us. There's Lucie, eyebrows furrowed, ballpoint pen at the ready in her slender hand. There's no smog today. We sang "Down by the Riverside" in French today. The Pep Club met today. We graphed a quadratic equation today. Stop already, and let me wait. Wait for Larry to throw a line from Lenny Bruce as we leave the room. Wait for Jack to call out, "Say hey, Willy," when he passes my locker. Wait for next weekend's hootenanny. And wait for the junior prom. Lucie's going with me; I finally asked, and now I'll invite her to the fall play. *Our Hearts Were Young and Gay* won't open until November 22, but I want to make sure she's free. Stop and don't waste the wait, because, as one of our drama coaches says, "This moment will never happen again. Therefore, it must be perfect."

It was, but I didn't know it.

---

the patience to wait for the right moment and the courage not to be

Waiting in the Car

Sheryl L. Nelms

When Mom and Dad both worked at Boeing in Wichita, Kansas, they worked separate shifts. Mom worked the day shift and Dad worked the swing shift. Dad took us with him and left us in the locked car to wait twenty minutes alone in the parking lot until Mom came out. I was eight and my brother Eugene was five.

Eugene and I fought a lot while we waited in the car. Most of the time it was just verbal, except one time it got bloody. I stabbed Eugene with the barber scissors. I didn't mean to, it just happened when he tried to hit me, he hit the scissors instead. I was so scared. His hand was bleeding really bad. It looked like a red fountain coming out of his hand.

I was on automatic pilot. I didn't think about anything, except I had to get help for Gene. I gave him a Kleenex, and then I jumped out of the car and ran and stopped a man going through the security gate to work.

"My brother has been hurt," I said. "Please come help him."

He did. He got the bleeding stopped; then he went and got the security guard to come talk to us.

The security guard asked us a lot of questions, and then Mom showed up. She was really upset.

After that, Mom and Dad hired a baby-sitter to take care of us. No more waiting in that parking lot.

Ballad of a Coal Miner's Wife
Fern G. Z. Carr

Plant remains in the bowels
of a primordial swamp
crushed under sand and mud
transform from peat to anthracite
to sweat, to tears, to blood —

but these were not your thoughts
as your husband left for work
with his pickaxe, shovel,
miner's helmet and
a "Don't-worry-about-me" look
that betrayed his chiseled face;

when he returned home
you tried not to notice
the stooped shoulders and wheezing,
you ignored the coal dust
that camouflaged his features
and crept into his aching lungs
slowly suffocating him

like a black cat
stealing the breath
from a suckling infant

until the unmentionable
finally had to be mentioned,
judiciously —
meted out in whispers
and knowing glances
after his descent
down the mine shaft
hundreds of feet below
to lay explosive charges
that were never destined for him —

charges that commingled his remains
with the bowels of a primordial swamp
crushed under sand and mud
to transform him into nothing more
than a carbon-trace memento
whose final bequest
was a heart drawn in the dust
and an "I lov" scrawled
with trembling hand

while you set the dinner table
glancing at the door
awaiting your children's father
who can't come home anymore.

Waiting and Entering

Jennifer Clark

Scattered throughout the country are keys
waiting for hands that have hidden them.

Quietly, without complaint,
they pass the time —
resting inside faux rocks,
lounging on ledges and under dusty mats,
hanging from hooks and rusty nails,
sitting under the infamous chipped flowerpots
of this world.

When their time finally comes,
thin, grooved bodies
must be pressed into remembering;
they have to be jiggled, turned, cajoled,
and convinced to crack open
this moment for which they were made.

Waiting in Greyhound Depot on Spring Street

Al Carty

Got my duffel bag between my knees and I'm watching the parade of humanity mixing it up for my amusement and education. This Greyhound depot is the old one on Spring Street, the 1958 model, complete with competing pimps with their entourages of painted sweeties of all shapes, sizes and ages, some of the bloated old girls who won't be here next year, or maybe next month. One group passes close, the girls smiling their hatred, all encompassed in an aura of cheap perfume and knit stockings that are meant to hide the bruises.

Sitting in front of me, a black guy with a faded backpack that came from Army surplus has tried to shift the pack from one shoulder to another and has dropped the load, and the flap comes open. About ten wieners are rolling around among the cigarette butts and sour spit. He picks them up and jams them back inside the bulging pack and straightens his fedora that has a hatband that shows the stains of a lot of city summers. I thought it probably came from a trash can over on Central Avenue, maybe outside a Mercy Mission where the lonely hopeless gather and listen to the obligatory sermon, then eat the salty meal in grateful silence.

He hoists his load to his shoulders and goes by me, and I smell the ancient odor of the street, the stale-cigarette-and-sweat smell, like cold chicken soup. He heads out to the nighttime alleys where I hope he finds a safe spot to rest.

The speakers squawk with information that is garbled as the voice bounces from wall to wall and echoes through the crowded lobby. I finally hear the name of a small California town and wait for the door to slide open. Some other people stand up and shuffle on to my door, and I wonder how far they're going and how far they've come to get here. It makes me smile to think of that first bus trip and how long ago that was, but now I'm here. I button my Ike-jacket and look down at my boots that have had their last spit-shine and drag my gear on over to the door.

Just a two-hour bus ride, but after the ship and train, I can stand a little bus ride. I crossed an ocean and a country, so this will be that piece of cake you always hear about. I've been waiting to be right here for so long and now I'm here. The waiting is almost over. Soon my civilian life will begin and this memory will tuck away in a corner with the others that will be stories someday, to wait...until called for duty.

"*Light thinks it travels faster than anything but it is wrong. No mat-*

The Waiting Room

Fred Skolnik

Three months is not a long time. Sometimes they pass quickly, sometimes more slowly. Sometimes they are filled with events, and sometimes they are uneventful. And sometimes you find yourself exactly where you were three months before, as if time had not passed at all.

Dr. White's receptionist always remembered me, and I remembered her. She sat in the same place, in the same posture, and might have been wearing the same clothes, as if she'd been there all this time without a break. She smiled as she always smiled and spoke in the same tone of voice, and the patient ahead of me sat exactly where he had three months earlier and again needed to see the doctor for just a moment to renew a prescription.

The receptionist's name was Julie. I wondered about her, wondered if she was married, just as I had before. She was in her late thirties or early forties, still attractive and without a ring. The office was comfortably air conditioned. I tapped my foot on the carpeted floor somewhat restlessly as I always did, and Julie was busy as she always was.

I thought she might save time if she spoke more to the point instead of passing the time of day with every patient, but I realized that her friendly manner generated much goodwill and was as important to the doctor's practice as keeping appointments straight. But Julie was efficient as well as personable. She handled phone calls and dealt with patients without skipping a beat. Even when no one was on the phone or at her station, she kept on working, checking her computer, constantly updating the appointment book she kept in front of her. Clearly she was the heart and soul of the operation, the doctor himself a kind of appendage.

Two men came in and sat down opposite me. At the same moment I realized they were identical twins I remembered seeing them in the office before. Now the picture was complete. I had sat here three months ago, and three months before that, in precisely the same circumstances, and I could think of nothing of consequence that had occurred in my life since that time. In memory, of course, events can be rearranged, everything unremarkable swept aside so you are left with the highlights, so to speak...one doctor's appointment and then another...and nothing in between. In effect that is all that remains of life...things remembered. Otherwise we have only the present moment, perpetually unfolding.

It occurred to me that I could just as well not have lived between these visits. One visit could have been telescoped into another and I would not have been aware of the difference. Thus I could say that it did not matter if I was here now for the first time or the second time or the twentieth time. The intervening months belonged to a count being made behind my back, as it were. The passing of time did not belong to consciousness unless it was recorded in memory. I remembered only Julie and her smile, her voice, her movements, the room as it had been, and my random thoughts, which were always the same. *Time has really stood still for me,* I thought.

It occurred to me that in this way it is always possible to go back to another time. One must simply find a past moment that corresponds to the present moment, or vice versa, and erase the intervening days or months or years from memory. Then one could start again. *When I leave the doctor's office,* I thought, *I could have coffee in a little cafe I know and recapture the moment when I sat there years ago and dreamed of all the things I wanted to be. Even now, in the waiting room, I could go back to another time...when I first came to Dr. White's office and saw Julie on the phone and was attracted to her. I could flirt with her a little and with a little luck relive the months in a different way, take her to dinner and a show and get to know her better, so that when I came in now, her smile would be more intimate and she would whisper something to me and I might squeeze her hand.*

Julie poured a cup of coffee. The man ahead of me asked for his prescription. The twins talked to each other with great animation. *Here is my chance,* I thought. *Julie is unoccupied, that is, just having a cup of coffee and the phone isn't ringing.* I went up to her and was about to speak when the previous patient came out and Julie said, "You can go in now."

The doctor examined me as he always did, wrote out a prescription and told me to come back in three months. The twins were already waiting at the door when I came out. No one was in the waiting room for the moment, except Julie. I asked her to make an appointment for me in another three months. She handed me an appointment card. At this point a woman came in with a teenage boy. She went directly to Julie and they began to talk. In another moment, I knew, an elderly gentleman using a cane would come through the door. The waiting room would start to fill up and I wouldn't be able to talk to Julie again. I would turn to go and someone would say, "Is that yours?" and I would turn around again and see the cane on the floor. It was always like that. I must have been seeing the doctor for twenty years. We had all grown old and nothing had changed.

Too Late

Marian Gowan

I thought I would go, but a nagging little voice told me to wait a little longer. What if he shows up just as I leave? What if I'm on the wrong corner, at the wrong Dunkin Donuts?

It has been raining all afternoon, that cold, dank rain that happens in New England in November. The skies have been gray for days, matching my mood. I don't know why he hasn't called. At last a message, "Meet me at 3:00, usual spot." I assume this is the one he means, but what if he remembers a different one?

I order a second cup of coffee, a second coffee roll. I had asked for a "Dunkin Donut," the one with the little handle on it. The clerk batted her mascara-heavy eyelashes at me and said, "I've never seen those. It must have been a long time ago."

I guess it was. About as long ago as when I last saw him. He had arrived at the dorm one night and had taken me along with a couple of friends to Anthony's Pier Four, on the waterfront. That was the first time I had oysters on the half shell. Raw oysters sound horrible, but not bad with enough lemon and cocktail sauce, not to mention the

Dewars on the rocks. The waiter hadn't asked for ID, since we were with an older man.

I feel silly thinking he would show up again after all this time. He has his job in Georgia, travels to Boston only occasionally. He's married, trying to rewrite his own college days by hitching a ride on mine. Better to forget the whole affair.

I walk slowly to the door, open it carefully and glance down the street as I walk in the opposite direction. Is that his familiar stride coming around the corner? Too late.

Excuse Me

Melody Mann

Seconds meet and linger
   in the doorway,
   in no hurry,
   in heedless conversations.
I want to push rudely by;
   get a move on;
   get my groove on;
   get a life.

The Measure of Time

SuzAnne C. Cole

Measuring time, marking its passage by minutes, hours, days, months, years, centuries, millennia, seems easy. After all, our lives are marked by the passage of our particular planet around its small sun-star and its revolutions from light to dark and back to light again. We even have atomic clocks whose readings, from both the National Institute of Standards and Technology and the U.S. Naval Observatory, are guaranteed never to differ from Coordinated Universal Time by more than 0.0000001 seconds. And atomic clocks cost less than forty dollars at Walmart.

So who among us cannot measure time, cannot state accurately the day, hour, and minute, whether by atomic clock or digital? Our just-turned-four grandson, for one. Ripley has been studying space at school and has absorbed his lessons so well – "We live on a planet called Earth, Gramma, and did you know light bounces back and forth?" – that he's been promised a trip to the Cosmosphere, a Smithsonian-affiliated air and space museum in Hutchinson, Kansas. At 6:00 a.m. on the appointed day, he bounds into our room, climbs our high bed, and pounces.

"Gramma, Grandpa, let's go to the Cosmosphere now."

"Ripley," we murmur, "It isn't even open yet."

His lips tremble and tears escape. What does he know of atomic time? He does understand day and night, though.

"Go to the window, Ripley, and tell me what color the sky is."

Reluctantly, he pulls the curtain open and even more reluctantly says, "Still dark."

"Okay, what shall we do until the sky turns blue?" We three take turns making noises and letting the others guess what or who we are, we practice seeing who can stay quiet the longest (for Ripley, twenty-nine seconds), we tell stories, we exchange dreams (Ripley dreamed of hills, tigers, and presents – not linearly, but spatially, as images), and we wonder what we will see at the museum. Eventually we rise, dress, and eat breakfast. Although to him, it's been half a day at least since he got up, it's still not even eight o'clock. I read a dozen books to Ripley and his younger sister Louise; we craft some pipe cleaner and pom-pom insects and play a few rounds of Candyland until, at last, we load into cars for our forty-five-minute journey.

But as we pull into the Cosmosphere parking lot, Ripley's father decides we'd enjoy the visit more if we had lunch first. That's very hard news for Ripley. "Dad," he cries, staring through the rear window as the rocket display rapidly diminishes, "why are we driving away?" He's heartbroken until his barbecue sandwich with curly fries and pink lemonade is set before him. Then he devours his meal before asking, "Cosmosphere now?"

He breaks into a huge grin as all the adults say, "YES."

The day is a success. He sits in a bomber ejection seat, wants to be told the story of Apollo 13 two times over, and is saddened by the fate of Laika, the first animal in space, who died a few hours into her flight. He doesn't even ask about the gift shop, but when Gramma offers a visit there, he chooses a five-piece play set including rocket, shuttle, astronaut, moon rover, and satellite, while Louise opts for a small bear dressed as an astronaut.

At home Ripley and I play "space," checking the weather satellite, counting down to blast off, landing on the moon, loading moon rocks, and returning safely to earth. ("Not like the doggy Laika, right, Gramma?") At nighttime, he carefully packs the space set into its box and takes it to bed with him.

The next morning, again not quite dawn, he's on our bed. "Gramma, Grandpa, guess what? In the night I couldn't find my space set, and I was so, so sad, but then I got up and looked on the floor and there it was – it fell off." I sleepily congratulate him for not waking a grownup to aid in his search. "I know, Gramma. I was good. Now can we go back to the Cosmosphere?"

"Not today, Ripley. But we'll try to go again. Would you like Gramma to make oatmeal with raisins?"

"And brown sugar?"

"Of course."

"And a marshmallow?"

"You're pushing your luck, kiddo. Marshmallows after lunch."

"When's lunch?"

Is it too soon to teach Ripley to tell time?

Poet in the Waiting Room

Barbara Darnall

I cannot not listen
so I eavesdrop shamelessly,
drinking it all in
against the drought when
words are scarce and
ideas nonexistent.
A hefty blonde chatters on
and on about her back surgery
as though its outcome were
crucial to national security.

Across the way, an old man
chews his pencil as he
contemplates the morning
crossword. A baby frets,
unable to be comforted by
mother's croon, while nearby
a toddler plays, one eye open
for an opportunity to misbehave.
Strangers chat as friends might,
telling more than they realize
to ears unable to ignore
their small talk. A diverse
smattering of humanity
brought together by suffering
and the hope of relief.
I watch and listen, enthralled
by the rich parade of
unfolding stories, eyes and ears
alert to record everything, fodder
for the not-yet-born poems
incubating in my brain.

Barbara B. Rollins

the shortest line
motionless transfixed —
in homage to my presence?

Carlos Colón

awaited spider lilies
this year on my side
of the neighbor's shrubs

Carlos Colón

waiting for me
at the edge of the forest
my shadow

Carlos Colón

waiting for power
needing a flashlight
to find the flashlight

Waiting at its Worst

Sharon Ellison

Your loved one is ill. You know he or she will never get better, yet you hope. You hope they are not in pain. You hope you are letting them know how much you love them. You hope you are doing everything right. You hope you can maintain a positive attitude in front of them. You hope your anger and frustration do not show. Waiting for the inevitable is waiting at its worst.

My husband's illness worsened quickly over his last thirteen months. Fortunately, he was not in what most of us call pain. In fact, he became fairly irritated each time Hospice folks asked him, "On a scale of one to ten, with one being no pain and ten being severe pain, what is your pain level?" He would take as deep a breath as possible, set his jaw, look directly at them and say, "I am not in any pain. I just have a hard time breathing!" His response always made me smile. I would remind him it was in their job description, at which point he would close his eyes and slowly shake his head.

He had every right to be frustrated. He could no longer do the things he loved, like singing, cooking, yard work, fishing, tennis, and making his grand-

father, Jo. He never loses patience, never doubts or complains, but al-

children laugh. By then, the only thing he could control was the TV remote.

The only time I heard him complain during his last thirteen months was about my cooking. He essentially gave me lessons during those months... not that I couldn't cook; I just didn't cook as well as he. He also gave me lessons about taking care of the yard and garden. I admit to having been a bit overwhelmed in the yard and garden area since he left.

I hoped his death would not be soon. I did my best to remain positive in front of him, but inside I was angry at his illness for taking away the abilities of the man I loved and for stealing our plans for... well, just plain living. Three months before his death, he assured me he was prepared to go whenever God called him home, but said he wasn't ready to leave me, or the children and grand-children. None of us were ready for that, either.

A year ago when he slipped peacefully into eternity, his last word was, "Bye." No pain; no fear; just a peaceful, "Bye." Breathe easy, my love.

Once again I was waiting: for family, friends and the funeral home. I was numb...no pain on that scale of one to ten. Just another round of waiting at its worst.

ways hopes, and works and waits so cheerfully that one is ashamed to

Crossings

Carol McAdoo Rehme

She was death's handmaiden.

And Sue took the job gladly. The hushed night hours lent a kinship to her caretaking. A dim lamp haloed the bed with its circle of light, almost pulsing with the patient's measured breaths. Some saw this as a deathwatch. Sue saw it as a ritual journey, and she was merely there to attend to the boarding pass.

The thick soles of her worn, comfortable shoes padded across the room. Sue smoothed the bleached bed sheet, tucked in the man's thin blanket, and gently straightened his head to a more comfortable position. She plucked spent blossoms from a vase of daisies, tidied the hospital stand, and scooted a vinyl chair closer to the bed. The oak frame groaned as she sank her ample weight into it.

The end wasn't always peaceful. Sometimes it arrived with distress, pain, and fear but – more often – the opposite was true. Either way, families wanted someone in attendance and, for one reason or another, many couldn't be there themselves. For some it was simply too painful; others couldn't spare the time or bear the wait; a few families lived too far away.

That's why Sue had replaced her cozy retirement slippers with her old nursing shoes. To tend the dying for the living. She felt comfortable volunteering to sit with terminally ill patients between the deep, holy hours of midnight and morning. She rarely slept well at home anyway. And it felt good to be useful again – especially with a patient like this one.

She and Arnold Taylor went way back. Why, they had attended the same schools, the same church, the same potluck dinners, and the same weddings and funerals in this small Iowa town. So it was only fitting that she attend his death, and Sue knew it wouldn't be long. She recognized the signs: his skin was mottled, his hands and feet discolored. And, since tonight's shift began, she'd already seen a change in his breathing.

The patient shifted slightly and moaned.

"It's okay, Arnie." Sue's strong, corded hand blanketed his, gently stroking the parchment skin.

His eyes, as pale as a work shirt that had suffered too many washings, opened and stared beyond her.

"You've had a good life, Arnie, but there's an even better one waiting." She reached over to caress his grizzled cheek. "When you're ready, Arnie, just cross over. It's okay. When you're ready."

And then it happened.

that have never bothered to bloom when we should have bloomed and

She felt it at almost the same time as she witnessed it: his wide-eyed look of radiant joy and then his hands reaching toward a presence. Sue glanced hopefully at the foot of the bed, all the while knowing she wouldn't see anyone there. She never could.

Then it came, an almost tangible release – as soft as the tiny last sigh that puffed from Arnie's smiling lips while his arms sank back to the bed. Expelling her own pent-up breath, Sue's trembling fingers brushed his eyelids closed.

Glancing at the clock, she noted the time, then paused to feel once more the solemn sacredness in the moment. Fleeting yet perceptible. Hopeful and holy. She felt privileged to witness it.

With a farewell glance toward the bed, Sue pulled a list from her pocket. Names. Telephone numbers. Now there was an entire family waiting, a family to notify, to console.

She was life's handmaiden.

Jane Blanchard

one could do much worse
than to lie low and fallow
until next season

it is as if the sun has become disgusted with waiting" *Charles Bukowski*

"No news is good news..."

Mary Carter

                    is mainly a lie.
Who do you know doesn't want a reply...
who wouldn't rather know something than not?
Waiting, the college where patience is taught,
is my alma mater and I know it well...
a dimly-lit hallway right outside of hell.

Not knowing's the torment...the sword overhead,
nightmare speculation on which fears are fed.
Better to see then, with truth's piercing light,
monsters or mayhem...get ready to fight.
Give me the bad news...yes, I'll take it straight!
Tell me the worst but please don't make me wait.

Empty Hours

Sheryl L. Nelms

tick tick tick tick tick tick tick tick tick tick tick tick

~ § ~ *"Do not wait for the last judgment. It comes every day."* Albert

Maybe Next Time
Madonna Dries Christensen

Sweet William – I'm your grandmother. I held you as a newborn, eight pounds, four ounces, twenty-one inches. That's considered a big baby; still, you seemed tiny, as babies always do. You had dark hair, blue eyes, and dimples that dazzled the nurses. Your sisters gathered around for a look. They knew you were joining the family, but with Grace just turned four and Sarah not yet three, they weren't sure what to make of your presence and the attention you garnered. Photographs reveal Grace's puzzlement and wide-eyed wonder.

Within a few months, you were solid; too heavy for me to lift.

As time passed, a year, and beyond, your development was not typical for your age. You hadn't babbled or tried to speak; your motor skills were delayed.

Friends offered:

Boys develop slower than girls.
He'll catch up.
My brother didn't talk until he was past three.
Have you had his hearing checked?

These are all valid comments, and often prove true. Doctors advise parents not to compare one child's milestones with another's, regardless of chronological age. As long as there's progress, to each his own stride.

Still, some children require further observation. You underwent tests for this, that, and the other. We heard the phrase *on the spectrum*, and learned that it covers a host of disorders from severe, to mild, to high-functioning. Viewed through rose-colored lenses, *on the spectrum* was a comfort – a rainbow with a positive outcome.

The diagnosis was autism. And sensory processing disorder.

Well, this wasn't your family's first challenge. Sarah's Down syndrome had been expected and we armed ourselves with information and resources. After recovering from heart surgery, her early intervention included physical therapy, occupational therapy, and speech therapy. Your parents had high expectations, and Sarah moved forward with enthusiasm and determination. She recently made the honor roll in third grade.

You're past six years old now, a handsome boy, above average tall, with a slender frame and a charming smile. You attend the public school's Multi-Intervention Program for students with Autism (MIPA). Your test scores are high. Your teacher says you are creative, determined, resourceful, and you like pranks and jokes. Your behavioral therapist

gray. A pale, in-between color. It reminds me of waiting for something

says you are really, really smart. Your occupational therapist swears you are a genius. Your speech therapist says you are the kind of kid who will take apart a computer to see how it works and then put it back together. These professionals and your parents understand your potential and work together to guide you toward goals they feel you will achieve.

For me, autism is a mystery so complex that what I've learned would fit in your sippy cup. You like being outdoors, especially on swings. You are drawn to clocks, the color red, stop signs, octagon shapes, and the number eight. You carry a blue octagonal wooden block with the number 8 on it. It's your lovey, your comfort object, like some children have a security blanket or pillow. You rely on stims (self-stimulatory behavior) to help manage sensory input from too much noise, light, or activity, as well as emotions: fear, anger, anxiety, and frustration at being nonverbal. Your personal stims include flicking lights on and off, and the motion of a wheel spinning or a ceiling fan whirling.

You communicate using a notebook filled with individual Velcro pictures and words, and an iPad. I'm grateful for the technology that assists you in socializing and gaining independence.

You've never seen Mr. Rogers, but on his television show during your parents' childhood, he promised children, "I like you just the way you are." As a child, his grandfather told him, "You've made this day special by being you. I like you just the way you are." That's how your family feels about you. We enjoy your company at any given moment.

This is not to say I'm immune to wishful thinking. I have muttered: *It's not fair,* quickly followed by*: For whom, then, would it be fair? A child who is out of my view, someone I can forget?* Yes, I wish your life were ordinary, but no child is completely protected from harm's way or problems. If it weren't this setback, it might be another.

Your sisters call me Granny. When Grace first began chattering, the word came out as Shranny. Sarah's speech was somewhat delayed but she, too, eventually managed Granny. Thus far, you have no sign language for the words Granny or Grandfather. You sometimes take my hand, or Grandfather's, and show us what you want. That means you understand who we are and that you trust us.

We make overtures, but wait for you to decide. On a visit I picked up a wooden puzzle whose pieces lay strewn on the floor. I gave you a truck shape and you placed it correctly. I offered another piece, but you'd already found something more interesting and moved on.

Maybe next time you'll play longer.

You entertain yourself from early morning until you fall asleep exhausted – often you awake only a few hours later, fully active. You use all five senses to explore and understand your surroundings. You switch on ceiling fans and watch the blades whirl; you flush toilets and examine water swooshing away; you turn on faucets and feel the water, then watch it flow down the drain; you scratch an oil painting to feel the texture and hear the sound your fingers make; you chew the pages of a book.

When you leave for school and are prompted to say "Bye" to me, you sometimes say "Buh," or give a small wave.

Sometimes not; you're focused on the bus, which you love.

Maybe next time you'll wave.

Maybe later you'll say, "Bye," and later still, "Bye, Granny."

More than once in a dream, I've been delighted to hear you speak. I excitedly tell someone what you said. When I awake, I can't recover the dream voice.

Maybe next time I'll capture it.

Maybe soon I will hear your actual little boy voice.

I'll wait – no matter how long the hours.

Maybe you'll bring a book and ask me to read. You're too big for my lap, but you will sit close to see the pictures and the words.

If that doesn't happen, it's all right. I will hold you in my dreams, thoughts, heart, and prayers.

I love you just the way you are.

you put yourself on a kind of track that has been there all the while,

Disturbances

Carolyn Dycus

Thoughts tumbling —
Falling through sleepless cracks.
Late night disturbance.

Hold on – slow down – wait.
Wait on what?
Questions rise in the dark.

Wait too long – life is gone.
Treasures slipping away,
Never mine to keep.

Wait on the Lord – hard.
One thousand years, a day to Him.
But not to me.

The Nursing Minute

M. Elizabeth Forest

Barbara pushed the call button that lit up the small light at the nurses' station and waited. She didn't like living on the second floor of the convalescent home; it meant she'd lost many of her privileges and privacies. Everyone knew that when you moved to the second floor, you couldn't take care of yourself. The primary condition for remaining on the assisted living level was the ability to toilet yourself. Barbara was embarrassed when they moved her upstairs; she was a woman of great pride and personal independence.

Barbara Fuller had been a school teacher, guidance counselor, and principal at Greenbelt High her entire life. Her career was her achievement, and she had little patience with waiting for her promotions as she climbed to the top of her field. Barbara taught thousands of young men and women (children, really) about the glory of achievement, the fast track to success, and the necessity of higher education. She had no time for slackers or underachievers.

"What's wrong with these kids?" she complained to her colleagues. "What are they waiting for?

Opportunities pass them by while they sit idly dreaming. How can I instill in them the need to get ahead and plan their future? I never waited for success; I went out and took it!" Her intolerance developed into a deeper contempt. "I made them sit and wait, thinking about their wasted lives." She kept them waiting in her outer office until they'd paid for their lack of ambition with some arbitrary amount of time that was an unspoken punishment.

Barbara pushed the call button again and waited. She knew that once the light was lit at the nurses' station and outside her door, pushing it again made no difference. Someone had to see it in order for the button pushing to be effective. Her face flushed red with impatience. *Why isn't anyone coming? It's been more than ten minutes. I really have to go.*

Since her stroke, she had lost control of her arms and legs. Sitting up...pushing the covers aside...swinging her legs over the side of the bed...and walking across the room, these were little things that had become big obstacles to her independence. She pulled up on the muscles around her bladder trying to hold back her urgency to go. She pushed the button three more times. *Why don't they come?*

A young woman popped her head around the door, "I'll be with you in a minute Mrs. Fuller. I'm helping Mr. Johnson, I can't leave him now." The nurse's aide reset the call button that switched off the light, then closed the door.

Barbara Fuller had spent a lifetime teaching and directing the lives of her students and staff. She expected their attention and respect. Now, for some reason, nobody listened to her. They didn't realize she was more important than whoever else they were attending to. *What's the matter with these people? Some of these girls aren't much older than my students. Who do they think they are, treating me this way?*

She pushed the call button again. "I really have to go!" she called out. "Is anybody there?" Other than the din of television sets up and down the hall, there was nothing, no reply. "Hello! Is anybody there?" She glanced at the clock on her bureau ticking away the minutes.

When they moved her upstairs, her family had come and removed many of her personal items. *They took away my jewelry. They took away my best clothes – expensive, tailored suits. The Director said I couldn't expect the staff to remove fitted slacks over diapers.* "Diapers! They're not diapers, they're adult incontinent pads. How insulting!" she muttered to herself. *And that Director, what an annoying woman, telling me, "You wouldn't want to soil such expensive clothes, now that you can't control your functions."*

"My Functions!" she said loudly. *That really boiled me. What difference does it make at this*

~ § ~ *"The only time to eat diet food is while you're waiting for the point if I soil my slacks and throw them out? They're mine! I can do what I please with them!*

She rapidly pushed the button and pulled up on her bladder in one final effort and then let go. There was nothing she could do. The warm liquid drained from her bladder and filled the pad, "Ahhh." she moaned with relief. Her hand went limp around the call button, at least there was comfort in finally being able to let go.

Barbara lay there soaked in her urine, which was becoming sticky, cold, and uncomfortable. When the smell reached her nostrils, she reached for the cord. "Where the hell is that girl?" she said loud enough for anyone to hear. But no one came. She listened. She could hear the sound of wheels moving through the hall. The nurse is coming with the medication. *Now I'll get some help. There's no point waiting for these girls who don't give a damn. It just proves what I've always said...higher education makes for the proper work ethic.*

The nurse opened the door, "Good afternoon, Mrs. Fuller."

"I've been pushing this button for a long time. Why can't I get any help?"

The nurse switched off the call light and walked briskly into room 219. "You need to wait, Mrs. Fuller. I have thirty-two residents who all need their medication. You must learn to be patient."

Barbara tried to explain, "I..."

Before she could utter another word, the nurse lifted her head and tossed the meds from the paper cup into her mouth. "Now swallow," she demanded as she poured the water into Mrs. Fuller's open mouth. "Be a good girl, swallow them all." The nurse glanced at her watch as she held Barbara's head.

The pills stuck in her throat, circles and ovals and football shapes all tossed in and pushed down with a rush of water. She choked and coughed. The nurse patted her on the back.

"Are we having trouble swallowing today?" She doused Barbara's throat with another rush of water and watched the pills go down in a reflexive swallow. "Good job, now that wasn't so hard, was it?"

Barbara barely finished the second sip of water when the nurse exited the room. "Nurse!" she cried out. No answer. The nurse had already closed the door.

The wheels of the med cart squeaked as it rolled down the hall to the next set of rooms. Frustrated, wet, and cold, Barbara pushed the call light again and waited.

"Nurse, Nurse... Hello? Is anybody there?" she yelled as loud as she could, but no one answered. The call light was on, but she grew tired of pushing the button and left it lying on the bed. She checked the clock; it had been forty minutes since she first pushed the button.

What the hell! I'll teach them to ignore me! She had an idea. She picked up the remote and switched on the television. *I'll just watch a little TV.* She laughed and turned the volume up as loud as she could. *Now I'll get some action!*

It was no time at all before a heavy-set, older woman, dressed in the familiar navy slacks and colorful hospital top the nurse's aides wore, came in and switched off the call button, turned down the volume on the TV and approached her bed.

"Finally! I've been waiting for hours." She felt the exaggeration would give impact to her statement.

The woman put the remote on the bureau, out of reach. "You'll bother the other residents if you leave the volume up that loud. Call me if you want to change the channel." She glanced back over her shoulder and smiled at Barbara as she left the room. "I'll check on you later, I just came on duty. I should be back in about an hour."

Barbara realized her mouth was hanging open, a big gaping question mark. She wasn't used to waiting; she was used to making other people wait.

Her skin felt cold and clammy; it burned. *Why won't anyone help me? Nobody can be that busy.*

Hundreds of young faces flashed before her eyes as she remembered students she'd kept waiting in her outer office so many years ago. Shy faces, and sad faces, faces filled with anger and tears, faces marred by deep and painful loneliness.

"Why do you haunt me?" she whispered.

Barbara closed her eyes, but they were still there, countless faces of young people whose deeper needs she never noticed.

"I had my own career to think about."

One of them spoke. *You looked but you didn't see. All we needed was kindness and understanding. Isn't that what you need, now?*

Looking for the Packard

Barbara B. Rollins

He'd always been decisive,
field-promoted to lieutenant colonel,
then mayor and business owner.
Now decisions were made for him
as he paced nursing home halls
speeding a wheelchair by scooting his feet.
Finished with the foolishness
he had a plan of escape
as soon as Mom and Pop
drove up in the Packard.

Catatonic

Bobby Samson

They say it's my birthday, thirty-two.
Then I've lain here a dozen years
tied to tubes, mute, immobile.
They speak as to an infant,
fawning over me. And mummer
to newcomers "collision"
"medical malpractice"
"policy limits" "gifted pianist"
then of my step-sister
"guardian" and "grasping, greedy."
Happy birthday. Indeed...
the best they might do for me,
my most fervent wish,
is release, death, finality.

Father Figure

Lisa Marie Lopez

Davey rests a gentle hand on my back and tells me everything is going to be okay. Mom nods with a soft sigh as I slip my father's letter into the pile of junk mail that clutters the kitchen table.

I have never met my father. I know nothing about him except that he's spent most of his life behind bars and spells my name, Savannah, with only one n. He plans on visiting me Friday.

Davey, who's been with my mom for six years, isn't thrilled with my father's surprise visit. He calls him a bum and a loser and every other name in the book.

Davey's a good man with a bushy red beard and a knack for fixing anything that's broken. He gives the best bear hugs and advice known to man. When Fred Lewis stood me up at the sixth grade dance, Davey stayed up with me the entire night, sharing stories of his own heartaches. We ate Rocky Road ice cream straight from the carton and watched *Full House* until the sun came up.

Friday morning finds me fumbling silverware and unable to eat scrambled eggs. I change my outfit three times and can't seem to find the right hairdo. All the while my head's swirling with all sorts of fears – *What if I'm not good enough for my father? What if I'm not what he wants or hoped for?*

I wait for him on the front porch. I read over my list doodled with things to talk about: pets, friends, hopes and dreams. All too soon, morning brightens into afternoon. Before long, I can smell Mom's spaghetti sauce cooking. Men in conservative-gray suits pull into driveways, greeted by elated children who jump into their arms, yelling, *Daddy's home, Daddy's home!* That's when it occurs to me my father might never come home.

I distract myself by going over the state capitals. Crickets keep me company with their songs. Whenever a car whooshes by, my heart jumps, but they keep going. After awhile, they stop coming altogether. Soon the sun sinks under the hills, and I'm left with only the crickets and starlit sky without a moon, or my father.

The front door screeches open and Davey appears. He asks if I want Rocky Road ice cream. I nod, blinking back tears. I feel worse than when Fred Lewis stood me up at the sixth grade dance. I tell Davey I was stupid to think my father would actually show. Davey cradles his arm around me. I bury my face in my hands and cry harder than I've ever cried in my entire life. Sixteen years of suppressed tears, set free.

When I peer up from my hands after what seems like an hour, the crickets have stopped singing and the neighbors have gone to sleep. But Davey is still there.

Redbird

Judy Callarman

I sat in my yellow chair near the window,
waiting heartsick for news of a death,
when a flash of crimson caught my eye —
a redbird perched on a holly sprig there.

He cocked his head, surveyed things below.
His bright assurance took away my breath.
Then he took flight, leaving me with a spry
glimmer of hope, lost but not relinquished.

~ § ~ *"Do not wait for leaders; do it alone, person to person." Mother*

Waiting for Spring

an anniversary poem

Mary Carter

Through bone-dry summer,
brown autumn, cold winter,
bulbs of crocus, runners of iris
guarded improbable color.
We waited; we hoped.
We did not know
we were holding our breath
until emerging flowers
made us sigh and tears of relief
mingled with spring rains.

Flying Solo

Kim Lehnhoff

Being a divorced parent sucks sometimes. After all the emotional warfare and the legal wrangling regarding child support and mandated visitation, I set about starting a new life with my six-year-old son, Daniel. I was dreading the approaching summer – and Daniel's first out-of-state flight as an unaccompanied minor. Despite my discomfort about the trip, I played the part of cheerleader as we packed his suitcase with his favorite clothes and his SpongeBob backpack with his most-cherished toys for the visit.

"Daniel, you're going to have so much fun with Dad! I bet he'll take you fishing and you'll get to play with Dad's dachshund Barney. Won't that be fun? It's only for three weeks – that's twenty-one days. I'll call you on Sundays, and you can call me anytime you want." I faked cheerfulness and told him that the minute he got back we'd do something special.

"Mommy, I don't want to go! You know I'm afraid of Dad and I don't like dogs. I want to stay home with you!" Daniel begged.

"Daniel, honey, you know you have to go. Let's both try to have a good time, and we can talk all about what fun you had when you get back!"

Despite his protests, he got into the car and we made our way to the airport. He received a lanyard with "Unaccompanied Minor (UM)" emblazoned on the tag – identifying him as my redheaded ship without me at the helm. The gate personnel were sweet and attentive and promised him a visit to the cockpit and a set of pilot wings.

When the flight was called for boarding, I gave Daniel a hug that I hoped was big enough to last three weeks and kissed the top of his head. "Be good on the plane and listen to the flight attendant who is going to take care of you. Call me when you get to Dad's, okay? I love you, Daniel!"

"I love you, too, Mom! I love you bunches!"

I handed the backpack to the attendant, and she took Daniel's hand.

"He'll be fine, Mom. We'll take good care of him. Enjoy your free time," the attendant said with a smile.

Daniel looked so small as he walked down the jetway, and my tears started to fall. I hoped he'd be all right and that he would have a fun time – but my heart already ached with his absence. I worried about how my hyperactive child would behave on the plane, and how he'd get along with relatives (including his own father) who didn't really know him.

ever for her, but that was before I found somebody else who'd give me

During my "vacation," the house was too quiet. I stayed late at work most nights during the week, getting ahead of deadlines. My brain was constantly distracted with worries about Daniel's situation, but I tried to soldier on. I ate out or cooked food that I'd never make if Daniel were home. Every single time he called on the phone, he'd cry and say that he wanted to come home. I did my best to reassure him that he'd be back soon – and reminded him that I had a special treat planned for his home-coming.

I tried to enjoy my respite from maternal responsibilities. I spent time with my adult daughter, or went to the movies with neighbors. We'd sit up late on each other's porches, sipping Zima and listening to the crickets and talking about the eccentric characters in our neighborhood.

One week turned to two – and then, after twenty-one long days, our wait was over. It was time to pick up Daniel from the airport.

After I showed my identification and proved to the airport personnel that I was the guardian of a UM, I proceeded to his flight's arrival gate. It seemed an eternity passed before the plane taxied up to the jetway. I watched as businessmen and other passengers began filing into the waiting area, and for a moment, I thought that Daniel's dad had refused to put him on the plane.

That fear disappeared and was replaced with a new kind of anxiety when a male passenger walked near me and asked in a very loud voice, "Where is Daniel's mother?"

I sheepishly raised my hand and asked, "What did he do now?"

"Nothing bad," the man said, smirking. "He was just very...entertaining." Apparently, Daniel talked non-stop during the flight – no surprise to me; I was used to his constant chatter. One of the flight attendants let him use the P.A. system, and he welcomed everyone to Pittsburgh and then sang "Take Me Out to the Ball Game." The man added, "You have your hands full with him, don't you?" as he strode off through the terminal.

I looked back toward the arriving passengers and saw Daniel holding the hand of a young female flight attendant. Daniel was practically dragging the woman to me as he shouted, "Mommy, I'm home! I got to sing on the plane!" His small hand wriggled from the attendant's grasp and he ran into my arms for a hug and a kiss.

His excitement was palpable as he continued: "Mommy, thank you for the special treat! I saw it! You had fireworks because I was coming home!" I had a local town's festival to thank for the pyro-technics in the sky that night, but I let Daniel think that I was responsible for the light show. I could check "special treat for Daniel" off on my to-do list.

I thanked the flight attendant and took posses-sion of my son. "We'll talk about that later, Daniel.

Now we have to go to baggage claim and get your suitcase."

Daniel continued to yammer about the flight – and his visitation with his dad – as we waited for his suitcase to appear on the baggage carousel. We stood next to an older gentleman with a scowl on his face, and Daniel immediately started telling him that this was his first flight, and that I had arranged for the fireworks show.

"I know. I sat behind you the entire trip," he said gruffly. Somehow, I think his wait may have been worse than mine and Daniel's combined.

Karen O'Leary

family dinner —
she sits at the child's table
longing to graduate

The Judge Is Never Late

Barbara B. Rollins

As a lawyer they said so,
but one judge abused it
so as a judge I swore
not to claim the right!

I sat on the bench
some twenty-three years —
the judge was seldom late.
Yet lawyers drifted in —
and out, then in again —
as we threatened confinement
to get them together. I waited.
And waited...and wrote
nine-and-a-half books
while I waited.

Sweating It Out

Terry Cobb

My husband Lynn half-carried me to our car, which was parked in a pasture between the combine shed where the local 4-H group was selling food and drinks and the row of Port-A-Potties that baked in the sunshine. Lynn turned on the air conditioning. I leaned back in the front passenger seat and waited for blood to return to my head and for calm to return to my stomach. Between slow deep breaths, I asked Lynn how much longer until the bidding on the farm would begin.

"The auctioneer told me it should start at about three o'clock, so only four more hours."

I groaned. Not being able to handle the heat is one of my not-so-funny quirks, and that old fainty feeling it brings always hits me at the most inopportune times...like at a land auction where our dream farm was up for sale.

It had rained overnight and instead of clearing the air, it only added humidity to a sun-scorched August day. We had spent the morning strolling up and down the gravel driveway looking at the farm implements and hedge posts lined up for sale, and already the back of my blouse was soaked with sweat. I felt fine as we moved, but once we stopped to inspect a decrepit Massey Ferguson tractor, the bottom of my stomach fell and my head detached from my body. I seized Lynn's arm and he could tell from my grip that we'd best get to the shade quickly.

Once he'd settled me into the car, he said, "I don't think you ate enough for breakfast. Let me get you a chili dog."

My stomach revolted at the suggestion. I grabbed his arm. "Oh, please no. Just a 7-UP."

"You need something to eat."

"I beg you, NO chili dog."

He left and returned with a can of 7-UP and a ham sandwich. As I sipped my drink, we discussed the obvious.

"It's only going to get hotter," I said. "If I can't stand up, then you'll have to do the bidding without me."

"No," Lynn said. "I won't bid without you. We're doing this together or we don't do this at all."

We had outgrown our forty acres in Pleasant Hill, Missouri, and for the last two years we had been searching for a larger farm to raise more cattle. Our plan was to raise enough cattle so we could eventually quit our city jobs and farm full-time. We had looked at many farms in the Kansas City area, but they either were too expensive or didn't fit our needs. Three weeks earlier, we became intrigued with an ad in *The Kansas City Star* about two farms to be sold at the same auction in Mercer County, about three hours from our home. We drove up to see the farms and fell in love with the larger, 654-acre one. It needed a lot of work, but we could envision our red Limousin cattle grazing on its rolling green hills. We talked to our banker and made financial arrangements. This farm was all we could think and talk about. It became our dream and now my intolerance to heat threatened it.

"When you start to feel better, let's take some short walks, and maybe you'll get used to the heat and get stronger," Lynn said. "Besides, it will help kill some time."

After a while, we walked around in the shade of the combine shed. A son of the couple who owned the farm came up and asked if we had any questions. He said his parents liked us and hoped we'd get the winning bid.

My legs became rubbery again, so I returned to the car while Lynn checked to see how the bidding was going on the farm equipment. I couldn't rest for the worries that nagged me. Would we be able to keep up two farms and two city jobs for a few years? Would we be able eventually to leave our jobs and make a living off the farm? I reached into my purse and looked at the card on which we'd written our pricing and bidding figures. *What if we didn't get it? What if we did?* I looked at the clock in the car dash. It was only one o'clock. My stomach flitted like a butterfly.

Lynn returned and we sat with the doors open to let a small breeze through the car. The sun was low enough in the west to provide some shade, and Lynn had bought more drinks and food. A few folks from the neighboring farms heard we were interested in the farm and came over to introduce themselves and wish us good luck. They didn't stay long, at least not long enough to make the hands on the clock move faster.

After they left, Lynn and I sat and held hands. In 1992, there were no cell phones or iPads to play games on, to divert our attention or pass the time. We had the car radio, but neither of us wanted to listen to music. Instead, we talked about how we'd fix up the farm if it were ours. We didn't want to get our hopes up, yet it was so comforting to make plans together.

It was well after three o'clock before all of the equipment and the wagons filled with tools and grab-bag boxes had been sold. The auctioneer asked the crowd to gather at the combine shed for the land auction. Lynn looked at me and asked how I felt.

"I'll be fine," I said hoping I sounded more confident than I felt. My stomach still jittered and my legs weren't strong. But this was our moment.

The smaller 300-acre farm, in which we were not interested, was offered first. The bidding bounced slowly between two or three bidders until there was only one left. The auctioneer called for a break so that the last offer could be presented to the family for acceptance. Lynn and I returned to the shade of the combine shed and discussed the bidding action we'd just observed. The crowd murmured and stirred as we awaited the auctioneer.

When he returned, he picked up the microphone and shook his head. "The family declines the bid. No sale."

Lynn and I gasped. What if our best offer was not accepted?

The auctioneer moved to "our" farm. Clutching Lynn's arm with one hand, I focused on our pricing card in the other, hoping my knees and stomach wouldn't let me down. The bidding began. Back and forth we bid with a middle-aged bearded man who seemed much calmer and cooler than we were. When we had nearly reached our top bid, the auctioneer stopped and said we'd break for fifteen minutes so that the seller and the potential buyers could think about the bids. He set the microphone down and walked over to the family sitting in the shade of the combine shed.

Lynn and I stared at the price card I clutched. One more bid and we would be at our limit. We couldn't afford to go any higher. We wondered if the other buyer had met his limit, too. Could he be a plant to drive up the price? What if the family declined our bid? We were too nervous to leave our spot so we stewed in the hot sun and walked in little circles to keep me upright.

Finally, the auctioneer returned and resumed the bidding. When we gave our highest, our final bid, we held our breath and watched our competitor. I thought my heart was going to pound right out of my chest. The man looked down at the ground, shook his head, and walked away.

I grabbed Lynn's arm and held tightly as the auctioneer said that he needed to take the bid to the family and see if they would accept. Having witnessed the last farm go unsold, I held my breath. Too many people had gathered around the family for us to see if they were nodding or shaking their heads. We tried to listen for an indication of their feelings but could hear only bits of conversations from the crowd.

Whether it was from the heat or the anticipation, my energy was draining fast. I was about to sit before I dropped on the ground when the auctioneer strode to the microphone.

"Sold!"

Our dream had come true. However, it was still six more years before we moved to the farm. Our wait consisted of more sweat-soaked days, but this time we were clearing off brush, building fences, and replacing barns. Waiting, working, and sweating it out together is what has made our farm and our marriage so special. Twenty years after that scorching hot day in August, we still live on our dream farm.

Esperance

(from the French: hope)

Becky Haigler

mourning dove's nest
a blot in the wind-whipped branches
of a leafless mulberry in March
steadfast through three days of cold rain
back to the east wind ruffling her feathers
she holds on for her life
and the life of her little ones
holding on without assurance
of the storm's end
holding on
holding on without knowing
whether she can keep them
warm enough to break out
fed enough to fly
holding on because the alternative
is shattered eggshells

Quit!

Bobbye Samson

Some few minutes to four
time ceases orderly march
to drag, trawl through stagnant pond,
languid, sluggish, moribund.
Too late to start new projects,
the morning's irritating, boring,
or at a stopping point. Idle chitchat,
furtive games – computer if allowed,
on phones if not. Grocery list compiled
or talk of evening's game.
And clocks, watches, digital displays
fascinate all, bringing glances
time and time again.
The minutes inch by ticking off one
when surely five have passed.
Then finally, at long last, close enough...
Start to close it down, inch toward the door
ready for the charge to cars and freedom.

So, Now We Wait

Marian Gowan

Today is a day of waiting. First I take my pill, and then wait an hour before I eat breakfast. We go for a walk in the meantime, both for our health and to kill time.

It is Tuesday, laundry day. My husband puts the first load in, and then we wait for it to finish. We wait for all the laundry to be done before we take showers. We would probably have enough hot water, but why risk it?

Next I call the vet. Ripken, the dark-red Golden Retriever who came to live with us eight years ago, is still not eating, despite the antibiotics he has been on all week for his 105-degree fever. The appointment is set for 2:30.

My husband says, "Let's eat our big meal around one." So I start the oven and wait for it to preheat. He has suggested baked potatoes, fish, Italian bread, and salad for the big meal. He plans and I cook. I wait until 12:30 to put in the fish. Then I wait ten more minutes to put in the bread. I make the salad in the meantime, both for our health and to kill time.

their lives and then they wait for somebody to tell them that this isn't

Now I am waiting for 2:30, to take Ripken to the vet.

Then we will wait for 6:00 o'clock, when we pick up our neighbors and drive to Harrah's in Chero-kee, North Carolina. There we will wait for a good hit. We know we are going to lose, but we don't know we are not going to win. And so we wait.

We arrive home just before 1:00 in the morning, having contributed handsomely to the Eastern Band of the Cherokee Nation. I set the alarm for 9:30. The vet is supposed to call with the results of Ripken's lab work. Blue Cross/Blue Shield would have covered it for a human, but because Ripken is only a dog, we have to pay the $90. That explains why the vet did not order the tests right away.

We are up by 8:30, to await the vet's phone call. No walk today. The schedule is way off.

The phone rings. "This is Dr. Boatwright. Rip-ken's lab results are back, and they are confusing, confusing. The liver is involved, but his white blood count is normal. So we know it is not an infection, but maybe it's a malignancy. We can do x-rays and ultrasound to find out what's going on. If you can bring him in now, we will x-ray him over the lunch period."

So now we wait. Will they be able to do anything for him? My husband and I discuss options, if it does turn out to be cancer. Palliative care, chemo, radiation. Between us we decide we will do what-ever is best for Ripken. We are both leaning toward doggie hospice. And then I wonder, are we talking just about Ripken?

The following day, the waiting is over. Now we know. The phone call from the vet has come. Ripken has an enlarged spleen, lesions on his liver and kidneys. A form of cancer common in large dogs, especially Golden Retrievers and German Shepherds. Hemangiosarcoma. Do I have to learn yet another cancer term? They have given him a steroid shot to increase his appetite. We will make him comfortable. No point in doing exploratory surgery, since they know what they will find.

The good news is that we can bring him home. The vet says to watch his appetite; watch for any signs of discomfort, or change in behavior. Does he still wag his tail and get excited about going for a walk? Does he still want to chase cats? As I leave the vet's office with Ripken, I say, "OK, let's go home to hospice." It is my way of letting them know that I do understand how serious the condition is. One of the technicians says, "I lost my shepherd last year. I gave him anything he wanted, mainly steak. After all, he had been a good friend to me."

Now on the day after the news, Ripken has refined his diet to eating only raw hamburger. Can this hurt him? At this point, it really doesn't matter, does it?

Following the vet's suggestion, we buy liver. I discover I can boil it, so it doesn't stink up the whole house. I give Ripken one small piece, and he eats

quantity. For each one who begins to weep somewhere else another

it. Then another piece and another. Before I know it, he has eaten a whole pound. The iron must be good for him. I buy only two or three packages at a time. After all, I don't want it left over.

Each morning we awake and check Ripken's breathing. Did he die during the night? We have been warned that this could happen. We keep watching for signs that "it's time." So far, he eats the liver, some raw hamburger, provolone cheese, more liver, some dog treats. He barks at passersby. He walks in the field, not a run, but at least a comfortable walk. He is not in pain, or if he is, he has not told us. I don't feel as helpless as before, just waiting for him to die. We are making him comfortable; he is not suffering. But are we keeping him alive for himself or for us? Is he waiting, too?

Even If It Is Godot

J.J. Steinfeld

"What are you waiting for?"
you hear amidst the traffic
and all you can think is
Not another voice
always complaining
grumbling at the portents
and other voices

---

stops. The same is true of the laugh." Samuel Beckett ~ § ~ "I've

and occasional vision
that might alter one's day.

This voice is persistent
stentorian even
and tells you
"I am waiting for Godot"
and you smile to yourself
to your voiceful life
to your errors and blunders
this one-liner bewilders you
this echo of Beckett
but you ask openly
so everyone within earshot
can hear: "Is Godot waiting for me?"

A tap on the shoulder
you refuse to turn around
or abandon the portents
and other voices
and occasional vision
those you can endure
but you can't face
what's behind you
even if it is Godot
arrived at long last.

in the bleak midwinter

Becky Haigler

Winter burrows in
like small mammals
curling into a hollow,
buried for yearly death.
Shorter and shorter days
rush to darkness, one moon
rising almost before another
has quite faded. Chill creeps
into earth, houses, bones, eyes.
Wrapped in a gray shroud, even
the sun is cold. We, too, hurry to
the nest, pull family close, gather
what warmth we can from sharing
space; offer stories like sparks, like
mouthfuls of light that sing 'til night
retreats again and morning triumphs.

Always the Moon

Amanda Hamilton

The Moon is beautiful tonight. I wish you could see it. Funny, how even after all that's happened, it can still seem so gorgeous. I know I should hate it; everyone else does. I just can't.

They say we only have a couple of weeks left. I'm glad. I've gotten over the panic and helplessness that seems to have consumed everyone else. Now I'm just curious. They say we'll only be alive for a while, once the Moon and Earth collide. They say the impact alone will destroy almost every living thing within the first hour, and that the rest will be wiped clean within the day. They say there is nothing we can do but wait.

More people have been taking their own lives as the days go on. I don't blame them. It certainly has its appeal. When gravity ceased to exist, many people began to simply let go. They would release their grip on the ground below and float up into the sky like balloons. I've heard that the effect is like carbon monoxide poisoning, except that the freedom and weightlessness of flying is the last conscious sensation. They fly up until the air gets so thin that they drift off to sleep. I hope that's true.

I can't stand the thought that you might have suffered.

It took a while to get used to having my bed on the ceiling. It was scary for a while, knowing that the only thing stopping me from floating up into oblivion was that thin layer of plaster and plywood. But I can see the Moon so well from here, if I hang my head off the side of the bed and look through our big glass skylight. It's enormous by now, a translucent globe of pearl almost swallowing up the inky sky beyond, larger every day as it approaches. If I squint, I can see the shadows of the mountains and craters on the Moon's surface, gray against the chalky-white flatlands. There is no day anymore, only the Moon. You always loved the night better, anyway.

I keep our little red radio next to the bed. All that's left on the stations is static, but for a while, it was the only way I got any news at all. Over and over they would relay the same message. The tides were getting too high, that was the first sign. They went on for months about possible explanations and dangers but nobody listened very seriously. The oceans were engulfing land all over the world and it was getting colder every day. The sun was dying and nothing could be done.

And then that night came when the world took you away. I saved myself. I grabbed the handrail on the stairs outside our house but you weren't fast enough. You floated up with millions of others, filling the sky, helpless. I saw you over my shoulder against the Moon, your arms and legs outstretched and uncontrolled.

You got smaller and smaller amongst all those people and cars and things until you blended in with the crowd. Soon I couldn't tell the difference between you or any of the others and the thousands of scattered stars behind you. Then you disappeared into the night and all that was left behind were those tiny spots of bright light.

That was the first week the sun didn't rise. The Earth stopped turning as the sun's pull grew weaker and weaker. The night stretched on and on. I stopped going to work that week. Everybody did. We all knew the world wouldn't be around much longer, so what was the point?

And what is the point now? All I have to look forward to is a slow, inevitable end to my existence. I will watch as that gargantuan orb nears ever closer to our surface, hour after hour, day after day, until it eventually meets our surface. That fateful kiss will destroy everything. But I cannot let go just yet. I can't decide if it's curiosity or cowardice – maybe both – but something keeps me here, staring up at the inky black of space, waiting.

You've been gone a month now and I miss you every day. I will meet you again soon. Until then, there's always the Moon.

Arrival Time

Neva Schuelke

Was it in the first lusty twinkle
In your father's eye?
Or – when sperm met egg?
Did it happen when cells began
To organize?
Or – in the first beat of your tiny heart?
Was it in the moment your lungs
Matured enough for survival
Outside the womb?
Or – when you took your first deep breath
And let out a mighty wail?
I sit here watching you nurse and doze
At my milky breast, and...
I need to know.
When did you finally arrive?
I want always to celebrate that moment.

Waiting for Zero

Margaret Auguste

Infertility is all about the waiting. You wait to begin your treatments. You wait to get blood drawn every night and desperately wait for the results the following morning. Your eggs are measured every day and you wait for them to grow to just the right size. Finally, treatment day comes around and you wait for the 24 hours for the medication to take hold so that the eggs are finally ready for release. Then you begin the notorious two-week wait to get the results everyone wants – a positive pregnancy test.

And then – incredibly and unbelievably – you are pregnant! The wait is over and you are filled with joy and are high in the sky. Just as quickly, you fall down as low as you can possibly go. The pregnancy is over before it began. There is no heartbeat, no baby. You miscarry, you cry – you wait to try again.

December 12, 2007 HCG 4711

Can't try again until my hormone pregnancy level is at zero. Am fixated on that number – zero. I deal with my devastation not by crying or asking for help but by planning my next attack. My next treatment. This time I will not waste my time with simple insemination. I will step off the cliff and take on in vitro fertilization. But I can't try until my pregnancy hormone levels go back to zero.

Took misoprostal last night and miscarried naturally today.

Hormones at 1400 and now the wait begins.

December 18, 2007 HCG 3056

HCG on the way down.

Nothing to do but wait and wait.

While I wait, I try to focus on the treatment, on the new medications I will take, the new ideas that will make this work...eating pineapples, maybe acupuncture or hypnosis. But as much as I try to avoid it, other thoughts break through.

Infertility is teaching me lessons that I never knew, like platitudes are real. *Hopes dashed. Empty inside. Want to tear my hair out...*all feelings that are real as rain to me. I feel all of those feelings. *I often feel as though my heart is in my throat – another platitude.*

I am choking on my despair. I am so angry that I pace around the house and hit myself and I think I actually could rip out my hair but then – someone might notice. If my husband and the doctors think I am crazy, they won't let me do the next treatment, and I must do the next treatment as soon as I am at zero. So, I keep my mouth shut and wait.

~ § ~ *"Think for a minute, darling: in fairy tales it's always the chil-*

December 25, HCG 1400

The numbers are going down fast now. It is like there never was anything there. But I know better. Now, everyone has stopped talking about my tragedy. It is over in their eyes and I am "lucky" they all say, because it all ended so early that it didn't really "count."

"Sure," I say, "you are right." I can say this because I am not really present now. My real self is somewhere else – waiting and watching the clock. My shell is pretending to live – to go on with life. I go to work, I cook meals and I go back to the gym to get back in shape, I tell people. But, really, it is because someone on one of my infertility blog sites told me that exercise helps the HCG go down more quickly.

January 2, HCG 300

The HCG is almost nonexistent. Now I can get back to planning my next attack, with no reservations. I start to read obsessively and post on all four or five of my message boards and blog sites. I write constantly at work, on my lunch break, and in my house when my husband is not there or is asleep, so he won't know how much I am posting and reading. I transfer my waiting anxiety onto the message sites. I write on multiple sites, getting advice, giving advice, and waiting every minute to see how many responses I receive. I especially used to be a regular on "two-week-wait" sites. These are sites that women and a few men go on while they are waiting to see if they are pregnant.

Amazingly, there are also sites dedicated to people like me who are waiting for zero – waiting to try again. I am not alone in my craziness and it is not wrong – it is strong and right. Only these people understand me, because they too know what it means to wait.

January 10, HCG 5

The wait is officially over. I look good. My husband, my doctor – they all say so. I let them think whatever they want – as long as they don't try to stop me from trying again. I cut my hair and buy some new makeup to get ready.

Waiting is a part of life and it is a part of my life that I am willing to live with if that is what it takes. I wait for my new appointment when I will get my new medicine. I will start giving myself the shots tonight and soon I will take a blood test to check my medication levels and to get an initial egg-size check. Infertility is all about mastering the wait so it doesn't master me. Or maybe it did master me, but it doesn't matter because the wait is over and I can begin again and start waiting for hope again – for just one more chance.

We Will Visit Egypt

Marigold Brown

I wait for you to die. I pray for you to die. And I spend all my waking hours making your life comfortable.

The cells in your lungs are husks now. You cough up brown blood, sometimes red blood. Pain, a jealous mistress, offers no quarter: when I try to hold your hand in bed at night, you push me away, saying my touch is too painful. A cocktail of medicines provides little relief, only hours of dopeyness.

There was a time when we partook of each other's joys and sorrows. No more. Disease has robbed me of the man who was my lover, my companion and my best friend. Unfairly, it has robbed you of your very being. Your only concern is your pain and discomfort, your only conversation your symptoms. Thank God for sport on television, which gives you the semblance of an occupation.

Sunk in your chair, you mutter, "Oh, dear me," half a dozen times an hour, hour upon hour. It is easier not to listen. It is also easier not to argue over trivialities. Go with the flow, answer the same questions time and again, and shut my ears to your lamentations. Inevitably, switching off means that

~ § ~ *"Then I thought, boy, isn't that just typical? You wait and wait*

you say something important in a lucid moment and I fail to hear. Your annoyance is justified.

Yet you are aware of your dependence on me, and resent this. "You know what I mean, you must know what I mean. The oligarch, the oligarch," you rage, face contorted with frustration. Somewhere in your brain there is a connection, and I must play guessing games to find the word you seek.

The cure for your bodily ills has addled your brain. Mental confusion and paranoia are known side effects of your strong painkillers. They take you down paths I cannot follow. You refuse outside help, claiming that nurses and doctors are against you. You distrust even our children, accusing them of greed and disloyalty. For my part, I take refuge in practicalities. Dealing with the here and now is a bulwark against grieving for what might have been.

There are still flashes of the old you, the essential you, the love of my heart. Old photos prompt happier memories, but sometimes bring petty resentments to the surface. Daily, we grow apart.

When this is over, I shall visit Egypt. For both of us.

I shall hold your invisible hand when I look on the Great Pyramid of Giza, for four thousand years the tallest man-made structure in the world. Why did we never go there? Difficult to say, for life itself intervened. We were so busy saving money, house-buying, nesting, and raising the children that the years flew by until it was too late.

and wait for something, and then when it happens, you feel sad."

"Do you remember the summer we built the wall?" I shall ask your invisible shade. That summer, the first in our family home, stands clear in my mind as a time of hard work and happiness. We painted the rooms, one by one, and restored the furniture we bought in junk shops. Out in the garden, we made a low wall in a simple square around the purple lilac bush. Reminding ourselves that the builders of the Great Pyramid created straight edges in the featureless desert by aligning their bricks with the stars, we played at doing the same one clear night.

Our wall still stands, filled with soil and the plants that were our first nurselings. Last week I tried to entice you into the garden to see the daffodils flowering within it. Anger flared in your weak voice. "I'm too ill to go outside." If we watch a television documentary on ancient Egypt, you now choose to fall asleep in your chair. Perhaps that is easier than accepting your plight.

For both of us, I shall stand in the museum of Cairo and admire the tomb paintings that depict a human soul facing Ma'at, goddess of justice. In her presence, the human heart is weighed on the scales against the feather of justice. You were the heart of my existence and I know that your heart, your generous heart, will never be found wanting.

And after that? Simple: I shall will myself to die. Why wait? Our financial affairs are in order and our children are parents themselves. Willpower was not enough to rescue you, but it shall not fail me. Ma'at, goddess of fairness, cannot disapprove if I loosen my hold on life in the hope of finding you again in the hereafter.

Through That Door

Barry Basden

We sit in silence, magazines on our laps, mine last June's *Sports Illustrated*, yours April's *Southern Living*. Other times, other places. The beige walls groan, compressed by this day, this hour. Cracks may appear momentarily. Soon a young Asian woman in green scrubs will walk through that door over by the vending machines, holding test results. She will glide toward us in sensible white shoes, this day not much different from her other days. I take hold of your hand and stare across at those machines. No matter what, I'm going to want a Moon Pie and a big RC.

Still Waiting

Melody Mann

Wait up; don't wait up; *Waiting for Godot*;
Lie in wait; watch and wait;
Wait 'til the cows come home;
Wait a second; wait a minute;
Hurry up and wait;
Wait in line; wait your turn; wait on hand and foot;
Wait until the ink is dry;
Wait 'til you see the whites of their eyes!
Wait list; can't wait; wait until next year;
Waiting period; worth the wait;
Wait for the all-clear;
Wait for it; wait in the wings;
But wait, there's more;
Wait for the other shoe to drop;
What are we waiting for?
Wait, wait, don't tell me; wait with bated breath;
Wait tables; time and tide...you know the rest;
Wait until the last minute;
Wait'll I get my hands on you.
How do I ever get things done
When "wait" is all I do?

take a chance on someone, and by the art of commitment become soul-

About the Authors

Margaret Auguste is a school librarian, mother of four and writer from New Jersey. She grew up in Indiana, moved to California for graduate school and to see a new part of life. There she met her husband and moved back to the East Coast. She has written about culture, history, and society for children's magazines and anthologies. She published her first book on censorship this summer. Writing allows her to express her observations on life and the world at large.

Shawn Aveningo is an award-winning poet whose work has appeared in *Pirene's Fountain, Tincture Journal, Featherlit, Convergence, Survivor's Review, POETZ,* and *Savage Melodies & Last Call Serenades.* Shawn hosts a monthly poetry show in Folsom, California, and has featured in Sacramento, San Francisco, Sausalito, Seattle, and St. Louis, and hopes to entertain audiences in more cities that start with the letter "S." Shawn's a Show-Me girl from Missouri, graduated summa cum laude from University of Maryland and is a very proud mother of three. She is also a founding member of the performing group, Poetica Erotica.

Cathy Baker is an award-winning poet who delights in observing God at work in the nuances of life, and sharing those observations through writing, journaling, and blogging. She and her husband live in the beautiful upstate of South Carolina with their answer to the empty-nest syndrome – a pampered pooch named Rupert. Visit Cathy's blog at *www.cathybaker.org.*

Francine Baldwin-Billingslea is a New Jersey native who now resides in the Atlanta, Georgia, area. In the last five years she has found a passion for writing and in that time has been published in over 25 anthologies and several magazines and authored an inspirational memoir titled *Through it all and out on the other side.* Some of her credits include *Chicken Soup for the Soul, Whispering Angel Books, Bellaonline,* and the new anthology series, *Not your Mother's Books.* She is a breast cancer survivor and a second-time-around newlywed who loves writing, traveling, and spending quality time with her loved ones.

Barry Basden lives in the Texas Hill Country with his wife and two yellow Labs. He edits *Camroc Press Review* and is coauthor of *Crack! and Thump: With A Combat Infantry Officer in World War II.* He is currently working on a collection of compressed pieces related to war.

Carly Berg enjoys waiting so much that she sometimes declines her turn so that she may enjoy waiting longer. When she is not blissfully waiting in lines and waiting areas around Houston, she can be found waiting here: *carlyberg. weebly.com.*

Kat Bert is the Executive Administrator for a large hospice company. During her years of dedication, she has seen many things and heard many promises and has been witness to "The Angels Among Us." This short story is a sketch of the humanity at all our fingertips. Kat has been writing since childhood and has been published in nonfiction works on hospice. Kat currently lives in Southern California with her two dogs, three cats, and loving husband.

Jane Blanchard has earned degrees in English from Wake Forest and Rutgers, and she has taught both secondary and post-secondary students. She currently divides her time between Augusta and St. Simon's Island, Georgia. Her poetry has appeared in many journals, magazines, and anthologies in the United States and the United Kingdom.

side, waiting for a better time, leaving you numb and half alive."

Marigold Brown is a pen name. Sustained by memories of a long and happy marriage, she is now a full-time caretaker for her husband.

Tanya Bryan is a Canadian writer and poet based in Toronto, Ontario. Her work has appeared in the *TOK 4 Anthology, NY_____* and *Misunderstandings Magazine*, as well as online at *Verse Land, Drunk Monkeys, Underwater New York,* and *Three Line Poetry*. She loves to travel, take photos, and write and draw her experiences, which are often surreal and wonderful.

Judy Callarman lives in Cisco, Texas. She is a retired professor of creative writing and English at Cisco College and a grandmother of eleven perfect children. Her poems and nonfiction have won contests and been published in a number of newspapers and newsletters and in Silver Boomer Books' *This Path, From the Porch Swing,* and *A Quilt of Holidays; Radix; Passager; Grandmother Earth;* and *Patchwork Path – Christmas Stocking*. She has enjoyed being a Silver Boomer Books guest editor for *A Quilt of Holidays* and *Longest Hours.*

Kathe Campbell lives her dream on a Montana mountain with her mammoth donkeys, a Keeshond, and a few kitties. Three children, eleven grands and three greats round out her herd. She is a prolific writer on Alzheimer's, and her stories are found on many ezines. Kathe is a contributing author to the Chicken Soup For The Soul and Not Your Mother's Book series, *RX for Writers*, magazines and medical journals. *kathe@wildblue.net.*

Fern G. Z. Carr is a member of The League of Canadian Poets, a former Poet-in-Residence, lawyer, and teacher. She composes poetry in five languages and has been published extensively world-wide from Finland to Mayotte Island (Mozambique Channel). A winner of national and international poetry contests, she has had her poetry set to music by a Juno-nominated musician. Carr was recently featured online in the arts section of Canada's national newspaper, *The Globe and Mail*. She also has had the honour of having her poem "I Am" chosen by the Parliamentary Poet Laureate as Poem of the Month for Canada. *www.ferngzcarr.com*

Mary Carter is a playful Texas poet who declines to take herself or her work too seriously. She is the younger alter ego of a somewhat plodding and pedantic writer who would dance like no one was watching if she weren't so clumsy.

Al Carty was once a Californian but is now happily transplanted in the high plains of New Mexico. He grows garlic and chilis and roams the piñon-juniper hills and writes about the thoughts he finds there. He has been romancing the Muse for a long time. Sometimes she dances for him and sometimes she hides among his thoughts. Since he discovered that rewriting makes her smile (as well as editors), his stories and poems have been accepted by *Menda City Review, 5th Story Review, Written Word, Cause and Effect Magazine, Sage of Consciousness,* Silver Boomer Books, and others.

Madonna Dries Christensen lives in Sarasota, Florida, with her husband. Three times nominated for the Pushcart Prize, she pens a monthly column for *Extra Innings* and writes about disabilities (and abilities) for *Unique Me Magazine*. Her stories have appeared in Silver Boomer Books' *From The Porch Swing; The Harsh And The Heart;* and *A Quilt Of Memories*. She's the author of *Swinging Sisters; Masquerade: The Swindler Who Conned J. Edgar Hoover; Dolls Remembered; Toys Remembered;* and the memoir *In Her Shoes: Step By Step. www.madonnadries christensen.com*

Jennifer Clark lives in Kalamazoo, Michigan. Her first book of poems, *Necessary Clearings*, will be published by Shabda Press in 2014. *Failbetter, Main Street Rag, Solo*

Novo, Paper Crow, Fiction Fix, and *Dogs Singing: A Tribute Anthology* (Salmon Press) are a few of the places that have made a home for her writings. Her recently completed manuscript for middle schoolers is patiently waiting for the right agent.

Beth Lynn Clegg, Houston, Texas, is an octogenarian who began her writing career after retiring from other endeavors. She has been published in Silver Boomer Books, A Cup of Comfort books, Texas Poetry Calendars, a variety of anthologies, magazines, newspapers, and elsewhere. Her essay "American Democratic Ideas and Practice" won third place in a 2002 Bryan Writers Annual Essay and Poetry Contest and is in the archival collection of The George Bush Presidential Library and Museum. She enjoys cooking, gardening, reading, church activities, any time with family, friends, and two spoiled cats, Molly and Tex.

Terry Cobb resides with her husband on a farm in north central Missouri, where she gardens, writes, and photographs whatever catches her eye. Her short stories have appeared in *Bylines 2010 Writer's Calendar, Downstate Story E-zine* (2012), *Well Versed 2013 Anthology,* and she has devotionals that will be published in the Fall 2013 issues of *The Upper Room* and *The Secret Place.* Her gardening blog is at *whatsinyourgarden.wordpress.com.*

SuzAnne C. Cole is a retired college instructor, wife, mother, and grandmother. She and her husband have traveled and hiked the world, including Iceland, China, Nepal, Panama, Peru, Chile, Australia, New Zealand, Britain, Ireland, Argentina, and Russia. Her essays have been published in *Newsweek,* the *Houston Chronicle, San Antonio Express-News, The Baltimore Sun, Personal Journaling, Front Porch Review,* and *Troika* as well as many anthologies. She writes in a studio in the woods in the Texas Hill Country.

She's pleased to have had works published in five previous Silver Boomer Books anthologies.

Christine Collier is married, the mother of three and grandmother of eight, and lives in upstate New York. She is the author of eight books, including a four-book mystery series, *The Writer's Club, Mystery is our Shadow, Christmas at Cliffhanger Inn,* and *Something Borrowed, Something Blue.* Her newest book is *Solve a Cozy Mystery – 35 Mini-Mysteries with Solutions.* Life stories from Christine have been published in anthology books by Guideposts, Patchwork Path, Adams Media, HCI Ultimate Books, Write Integrity Press, Chamberton Publishing, and *knowonder!*

Carlos Colón is the author of *Haiku Elvis: A Life in 17 Syllables (or Less)* by Laughing Cactus Press as well as twelve poetry chapbooks. His work was recently anthologized in *The Southern Poetry Anthology: Volume IV: Louisiana* (Texas Review Press, 2011), *Haiku 21* (Modern Haiku Press, 2011), and *Haiku in English* (W.W. Norton, 2013). Eleven of his poems have been reprinted in *The Red Moon Anthology*, which yearly collects the best English-Language haiku and related works. Colón has published more than 900 poems in a variety of magazines including *Modern Haiku, Frogpond, Journal of Poetry Therapy, Writer's Digest,* and *Louisiana Literature.* He is also one of the poets featured in Tazuo Yamaguchi's *Haiku: Art of the Short Poem,* a DVD documentary. Follow Haiku Elvis on Twitter @ccolon423.

Barbara Darnall, the daughter of a high school English teacher and a West Texas lawyer and rancher, has been surrounded by words all her life and grew up telling stories and writing scripts for her playmates to perform. She graduated from Baylor University with B.A. and M.A. degrees in drama, and taught at the college level for several years. Immediate past-president of Abilene Writers Guild, she writes poetry, articles, and personal narratives, and has

just in case I have to wait on line for Santa, or some such inconven-

written and directed numerous short dramas for her church. She has copyedited one book and several manuscripts, and has published stories and poems in seven previous Silver Boomer Books anthologies. As a tax consultant for more than thirty years, she particularly enjoys the letter-writing contests she occasionally gets into with the IRS!

Elsi Dodge is a single, retired, Boulder, Colorado, teacher who travels with her dog and cat in a thirty-foot RV, co-leads a Bible study, works with a church youth group, and advocates for families struggling with the special ed system. Blog at *www.RVTourist.com/blog*.

June Rose Dowis reads, writes, and resides in Shreveport, Louisiana. A love of nature, a heart for the underdog, and a slice of everyday life find their way into her poetry that is divided equally between contemporary style and haiku. Her essays have been published in *Birds & Blooms, Appleseeds, Byline,* and *Shreveport Voices.* Her poetry has been published in *Ouachita Life, Acorn, A Hundred Gourds* and anthologies, *From the Porch Swing, This Path, The Harsh and the Heart,* and *Harbingers of Hope in Hard Times.* She was also a winner of the Highway Haiku Contest in Shreveport, with her haiku gracing a billboard.

Carolyn Dycus is a retired district court administrator, active volunteer, bookaholic, and lifetime journaler. Her varied works have included online devotional contracts, and even a *True Story* magazine article. She lives out her love of children's literature through years of reading to eleven grandchildren, and her love of history by serving as a docent to schoolchildren at a Texas frontier museum. She also advocates for women and children in developing countries through a local non-profit organization. Her daily challenge and focus is carving out quiet time for writing.

Sharon Ellison is a medical office manager and freelance writer who lives in Abilene, Texas, with her blonde

Pekingese, Judah. She has been published in several previous Silver Boomer Books anthologies as well as *Proceedings* and *Nostalgia* magazines. She has three grandchildren nearby and two far away. Along with writing, she enjoys reading, singing, playing piano, and traveling.

Renee Emerson teaches poetry at Shorter University. She has her MFA from Boston University and is the author of three chapbooks, most recently *Where Nothing Can Grow* (Batcat Press). Her work has appeared in literary magazines such as *32 Poems, Indiana Review,* and *Christianity & Literature.*

Wendy Estelle-Bialek has resided most of her life in Southeastern Connecticut. However, she is currently enjoying a nomadic lifestyle, living full-time in an RV while traveling throughout the United States with her husband. After spending nearly two decades in the world of administrative services, including a stint as a content writer for a web design firm, she ultimately ignited her writing career as a full-time reporter for a local weekly newspaper. Once the initial fear of knowing her work would be read by thousands of subscribers each week subsided, she was hooked. Today she uses her time traveling the country to write short stories and plans to publish her first novel in the fall of 2013. You can follow Wendy along on her travels as she writes about her gypsy lifestyle at www.AmericanGypsyGibberish.com

Wayne Faust has had over 35 stories published in various places, including one in Norway and another in Australia. He authored a full length, non-fiction book called *Thirty Years Without A Real Job,* recounting his experiences as a full-time music and comedy performer, which is still his full-time job. You can find out more about Wayne on his website at *www.waynefaust.com,* where you can read some of his fiction for free online and listen to funny songs.

Dare Freeman Ford is author of *Don't Make Me Turn this Bus Around,* chronicling her adventures as a teenage bus driver in Anson County, North Carolina. Her work has appeared in several Southeast regional publications and anthologies. A retired teacher specializing in special-needs students, she lives in Hendersonville, North Carolina.

M. Elizabeth Forest was a modern dancer who taught children the joy of movement and creative expression. She wrote poetry as a young woman and was published in her college arts journal. While living in New York, her career evolved to massage therapy and later, nursing. She is married and has raised three daughters. Stricken with chronic Lyme disease for more than ten years, she began writing fiction to express her creativity. She is a Lyme survivor now working toward publication in order to share her life's experience with others. She lives with her husband in New Hampshire.

Rosie Garland was born in London to a runaway teen-ager and has always been a cuckoo in the nest. An eclectic writer and performer, ranging from singing in cult gothic band *The March Violets,* to twisted alter ego *Rosie Lugosi the Vampire Queen*, she has five solo collections of poetry and is winner of the DaDa Award for Performance Artist of the Year and a Poetry Award from the People's Café, New York. She also won the Mslexia Novel competition in 2012, and her debut novel *The Palace of Curiosities* was released in March 2013 by HarperCollins. *http://www.rosiegarland.com.*

Nancy Gauquier loves to travel. She grew up in Massachusetts, and has lived in Vermont, Oregon, New York City, Seattle, and East Sussex, England. Her stories have been published in the U.S., Canada, England, and New Zealand. She now lives in central coastal California.

Sarah Geil is currently pursuing degrees in English and psychology at Shorter University in Rome, Georgia. Her poetry has been published in the university's literary magazine, *The Chimes.* In a different vein of publication, her research on birth order and academics has appeared in a Harvard scientific journal.

Marian Gowan, a graduate of Tufts University, discovered personal writing after retiring to Hendersonville, North Carolina, from western New York, following her thirty-year career in a large corporation. She is author of *Notes from the Trunk,* a memoir of her mother's life from 1920 to 1940, published by Old Mountain Press (*www.oldmp.com/mariangowan.htm*). Her work has appeared in several Southeast regional publications and anthologies.

Alice King Greenwood has been writing poetry, prose, and music since taking early retirement from teaching school thirty years ago. She draws her material from multifaceted personal experiences in travel, community involvement, and most importantly, life with her large family of five children, twelve grandchildren, and thirteen great-grands. Her compositions have won numerous awards and have appeared in more than four dozen publications.

Becky Haigler is a founding partner in Silver Boomer Books, a contributor to all the SBB anthologies and the author of *not so GRIMM: gentle fables and cautionary tales,* a collection of magic realism stories from Laughing Cactus Press. She is retired from teaching Spanish in Texas public schools and now resides in St. Louis, Missouri.

Amanda Hamilton was born in Columbia, Missouri, in 1990. She holds a BFA in Creative Writing from Truman State University in Kirksville, Missouri. She was recently engaged to her boyfriend of four years, and they plan to marry in May 2014. She can play a mean accordion and a decent ukulele. Her work has previously been published in *CC&D Magazine, Foliate Oak Literary Magazine,The*

Evansville Review, Menda City Review, Northwind Maga-zine, Echo Ink Review and *See Spot Run.*

Haiku Hannah is an observer, admirer, and would-be practitioner of modern English haiku. Until she takes the craft more seriously, she will remain anonymous.

Dixon Hearne, a Louisiana native, teaches and writes in southern California and Mississippi. He has been twice nominated for the Pushcart Prize and earned the 2010 Creative Spirit Award-Platinum, for *Plantatia*, a collection of 34 short stories. His work has appeared in several Silver Boomer Books anthologies, as well as *Louisiana Literature, Wisconsin Review, New Plains Review, Mature Living,* and many other magazines and journals. Hearne was a guest editor for *A Quilt of Holidays,* Silver Boomer Books' seventh anthology. His *Native Voices, Native Lands,* published by Laughing Cactus Press came out in September, 2013. He is presently at work on new poetry and short story collections.

Carolyn T. Johnson, a former banker and now freelance writer from Houston, Texas, writes from the heart, the hurt, the heavenly, and sometimes the hilarious. Life has provided many twists and turns over the years, but she subscribes to the advice of a popular Lee Ann Womack song, and when she gets the chance to sit it out or dance, she dances. Her work can be found in the *Houston Chronicle* and *The Austin American-Statesman* newspapers, as well as Chicken Soup for the Soul, the Whispering Angel series, Publishing Syndicate, and numerous other anthologies and e-zines.

Janina Aza Karpinska achieved an M.A. in Creative Writing & Personal Development at Sussex University in 2006, and won first prize in the Cannon Open Poetry Competition the following year. As *Ms. Merized,* she produced her own weekly community radio show of poetry; prose; music; and an audio book: *The Haunted Woman*, by David Lindsay (no longer in print). She is one of the usual suspects in I.D. Parade, a local Am Dram Company. She is also an artist and iconographer.

Charles Leggett is a professional actor based in Seattle, Washington. Recent publications include *Bottle Rockets, The Centrifugal Eye,* and *Big Pulp.* Others include 2012 Pushcart nominations by *Kansas City Voices* and *The Golden Sparrow Literary Review.* His long poem "Premature *Tombeau* for John Ashbery" is an e-chapbook in the Barnwood Press "Great Find" series, and his play, *The River's Invitation,* was featured at Seattle's Theatre Off Jackson as part of its inaugural Solo Performance Festival, "SPF 1: No Protection!" in March 2007.

Kim Lehnhoff is a wife, mother of three, stepmother of three, grandmother of eight and tech writer. She has been published in Mozark Press' anthologies *A Shaker of Margaritas: Hot Flash Mommas* and *A Shaker of Margaritas: Cougars on the Prowl.* Kim is President of the Writers' Society of Jefferson County, and a member of St. Louis Writer's Guild and Saturday Writers in St. Peters, all chapters of the Missouri Writers Guild. She enjoys spending time with family, reading, blogging, and taking roads to see where they go. Kim blogs at *The Ratio of Failures, ratiooffailures. blogspot.com*

Lisa Marie Lopez has had publications in *The Storyteller Magazine* and in various anthologies including *The Book of Mom* and *The Spark, Volume One.* She completed a course at Long Ridge Writers Group in 2012 where she was lucky enough to have author Lou Fisher as her mentor. She's had eight publications since and credits wonderful and inspirational Lou for making her a better writer. Lisa lives with her husband in Concord, California.

Melody was born as a young child and has lived her entire life. She currently lives with a *Mann* and has borne four Mann children. When not helplessly proofreading every billboard and cereal box she encounters, she earns a wage as a Tech Editor heroically rescuing dangling participles. She blames her career path entirely on her first grade teacher, Mrs. Campanella, who blithely inflicted literacy on over 35 unsuspecting children that year. Growing up in a military family, Melody spent untold hours waiting in one form or another, in one assignment after the other. A book or puzzle magazine was a more faithful companion than any pet could ever be and always spoke her language. She was delighted to pass the skill of waiting on to her four children. (One of whom still regularly causes her mother to practice late into the evening.) Having ingested a multitudinous amount of alphabet over the years, Melody thought it was high time to regurgitate.

Laura Matheson is just another mom, two little ones in tow, pencil at the ready, and camera in hand. Originally from the Canadian west coast, she now lives in rural Saskatchewan with her boys, her husband, and their two crazy English Springer Spaniels, and teaches communications and technical writing at Saskatchewan Institute of Applied Science and Technology.

John A. McColley lives in a vortex of worlds, characters, machines and language, constantly dragging images and forms out of the storm onto canvas, paper or computer screen to share them with others and give them new life. When not wrestling with words, he cranks dials and makes sparks at his local hackerspaces and searches the wilds of New Hampshire for semi-precious stones with his fiancée.

Anthony J. Mohr writes from his home in southern California. His essays, memoirs, and short stories have appeared in or are upcoming in, among other places, *California Prose Directory – 2013*; *Chicken Soup for the Soul – True Love*; *The Christian Science Monitor*; *Eclectica*; *The MacGuffin*; *War, Literature & the Arts*; *Workers Write!*

Tales from the Courtroom; Word Riot; and *ZYZZYVA.* He has appeared in *Freckles to Wrinkles, This Path,* and *Flashlight Memories.* His hobbies include hiking, travel, horseback riding, reading, and improv theater.

Claudia Mundell has a Border War in her writing. She grew up in Kansas, but her work life has been in Missouri. She has many memories from each state that work their way into her fiction. After raising a family and teaching, she now writes for pleasure – and maybe for profit someday. Her work has appeared in *MidRivers Review, Yellow Medicine Review, Rosebud, TEA, Good Old Days,* and *Romantic Homes,* and in several anthologies. http://claudiapagebookie.blogspot.com

Sheryl L. Nelms is from Marysville, Kansas. She graduated from South Dakota State University. She has had over 5,000 articles, stories and poems published, including fourteen individual collections of her poems. She is the fiction/nonfiction editor of *The Pen Woman Magazine,* the National League of American Pen Women publication; a contributing editor for *Time Of Singing, A Magazine Of Christian Poetry;* and a three-time Pushcart Prize nominee.

Karen O'Leary is a writer and editor from West Fargo, North Dakota. She has published poetry, short stories, and articles in a variety of venues. In 2011, she released a book of her poetry called *Whispers...* In 2012, she edited *Snippets...,* an anthology of poetry from 73 writers across the world. Both books were published by APF Publisher and are available at *www.lulu.com.* Karen is currently the editor of an online poetry community called Whispers, *whispersin thewind333.blogspot.com.* She would enjoy hearing from writers and readers at gksm@cableone.net

Martha O'Quinn currently lives in Hendersonville, North Carolina. She writes poetry and creative nonfiction. Her work has appeared in a number of anthologies from Old Mountain

Press in Sylva, North Carolina, as well as regional publications including *wnc-woman* and three anthologies edited by Celia Miles and Nancy Dillingham. Born in North Carolina, Martha has lived in five different Southern states and her writing reflects her true southern heritage. She is a mother of two, grandmother of four, and great-grandmother of one.

Carl "Papa" Palmer, twice nominated for the Micro Award in flash fiction and thrice for the Pushcart Prize in poetry, has been published in five previous Silver Boomer Books anthologies. He grew up on Old Mill Road in Ridgeway, Virginia, and now lives the good life in University Place, Washington. MOTTO: Long Weekends Forever.

Patricia Podlipec taught first grade for over two decades. After retirement she and her husband moved from Wisconsin to Hendersonville, North Carolina, where she enjoys many activities, including writing poetry. Her poems have appeared in *Kakalak, Clothes Lines, WNC Woman, Heart Journal, The Great Smokies Review,* and *Women's Spaces Women's Places.*

Carol McAdoo Rehme has survived The Waiting Place in countless ways with four children and ten grandchildren. A veteran freelance editor and award-winning writer, she is the author of numerous books. Her latest projects – a biography/memoir, *Finding the Pearl* and a delectable gift book, *Fundamentally Female* – were released in 2012.

Penny Righthand grew up in New York, went to nursing school in Michigan, studied creative writing in Washington State, and settled in Oakland, California. She worked as a journalist, but for the past 25 years has had a busy financial advising practice. She writes a column for the professional journal *Advisor Today* and had a piece in the Silver Boomer Books anthology *On Our Own – Widowhood for Smarties.* She works with her three grandsons on their pitching, dribbling and sometimes on joint writing projects. She's waiting to channel the next great American flash fiction.

Barbara B. Rollins, writer, editor, and publisher with Silver Boomer Books came to book crafting after careers as teacher, Christian educator, typesetter, legal secretary, lawyer, and judge. She started writing books while waiting for lawyers, and *Longest Hours* is the seventeenth book with Barbara B. Rollins on the cover. She writes a daily recovery poetry blog at *EagleWingsPress.com/daily*.

Ruth Sabath Rosenthal is a New York poet, well published in literary journals and poetry anthologies throughout the United States and internationally. In 2006, Ruth's poem "on yet another birthday" was nominated for a Pushcart prize. Ruth has a book of poems titled *Facing Home and Beyond* that can be purchased from *barnesandnoble.com; amazon.com;* or from Ruth via e-mail: ruthspoems@aol.com. She also has two poetry books forthcoming: *little, but by no means small* and *Food: Nature vs Nurture.* For more about Ruth, please feel free to "Google" her, and visit her website *www.ruthsabathrosenthal.moonfruit.com.*

Bobbye Samson hangs around, watching the ups and downs, triumphs and oops, of Silver Boomer Books, occasionally contributing a piece or two, just to keep the pot stirred. Her work is in *Flashlight Memories, Silver Boomers,* and *The Harsh and The Heart.*

Neva Schuelke was born and raised in the portion of northern California referred to as "Silicon Valley." Neva now resides in southern Arizona – where she belongs. Writing has been a primary form of self-expression since childhood. She discovered the short story form in her sophomore year of high school. Studying biology and, later, psychology in college, she has worked off and on as a natural science docent/educator and writer, dabbling in poetry from time to time. Mary Oliver and Billy Collins are two of her favorite poets. Journaling is a daily practice. She currently lives with a dog and two cats (all rescues) who like to help with gardening, crocheting and knitting projects. She still occasionally fantasizes that she will one day write the "great American novel," but the exact plot has not revealed itself – yet.

Elizabeth Schultz lives in Lawrence, Kansas, following retirement from the English Department of the University of Kansas, where she was Chancellor's Club Teaching Professor. She remains committed to writing about the people and the places she loves, in academic essays, nature essays, and poems. These include Herman Melville, her mother, and her friends, the Kansas wetlands and prairies, Michigan's Higgins Lake, Japan, where she lived for six years, oceans everywhere. She has published several books, and her scholarly and creative work appears in numerous journals and reviews.

Fred Skolnik was born in New York City and has lived in Israel since 1963. His novel *The Other Shore* (Aqueous Books, 2011) is an epic work depicting Israeli society at a critical juncture in its recent history. His stories, essays and poems have appeared in around eighty journals, including *TriQuarterly, Gargoyle, The MacGuffin, Minnetonka Review, Los Angeles Review, Prism Review, Words & Images, Literary House Review, Underground Voices, Third Coast,* and *Polluto.* He is also the editor-in-chief of the 22-volume second edition of the *Encyclopaedia Judaica,* winner of the 2007 Dartmouth Medal.

J.J. Steinfeld, Canadian fiction writer, poet, and playwright, lives on Prince Edward Island, where he is patiently waiting for Godot's arrival and a phone call from Kafka. While waiting, he has published fourteen books, including *Should the Word Hell Be Capitalized?* (Stories, Gaspereau Press), *Would You Hide Me?* (Stories, Gaspereau Press), *An Affection for Precipices* (Poetry, Serengeti Press),

lies waiting." Cormac McCarthy ~ § ~ *"Love's gift cannot be given, it*

Misshapenness (Poetry, Ekstasis Editions), and *A Glass Shard and Memory* (Stories, Recliner Books). His short stories and poems have appeared in numerous anthologies and periodicals internationally, and over forty of his one-act plays and a handful of his full-length plays have been performed in Canada and the United States.

Deborah Straw is the author of two published books of nonfiction and a college writing and literature instructor. She is also a wife, daughter, friend, and animal lover.

John Vicary is an author from Michigan. He's been published in various anthologies and magazines, starting with his first poetry efforts in the fifth grade. He's been the featured author at *The Petulant Poetess* and a ten-time winner of Brigit's Flame. He lives in the country with his spouse, five kids, six cats, two dogs, and a partridge in a pear tree.

Steliana Cristina Voicu graduated with a Bachelor's degree in Economic Cybernetics, Statistics and Informatics from Petroleum-Gas University of Ploieşti (Romania) in 2010, and in 2012 she received a Master's degree in Business Support Databases from the same institution. Her Romanian poetry and short prose have received awards in various contests and her poems have been published in Romanian anthologies. Her haiku have been published in *Ginyu Haiku Gallery, Diogen – pro kultura magazin, Ploc!* and *Asahi Haikuist Network*. Her haiku sequence – cold moon – received 3rd place in the Diogen International Winter Haiku Competition 2012.

Lois Kaskel Welch grew up in Delphos, a small town in northeast Ohio. She wrote, between the fall of 2006 and the spring of 2009, more than 35 short stories about her life. She was encouraged and supported by her teacher and fellow classmates at Writers and Books in Rochester, New York. Lois wrote about her early memories of life during the Great

Depression, her family's experiences in World War II, and her life as a young mother in post-war America. Lois and her daughter, Joyce Welch Nimick, were busy editing the stories into a book when Lois became ill and passed away on March 9, 2009. Her book – *Kaskel Family Memories* – was published in 2011.

B.J. Yudelson is a retired writer for not-for-profit agencies. Her essays have appeared in *Colere, Eclectica Magazine, Forge, The Griffin, Jewish Action, The Jewish Georgian, The Legendary, Slow Trains, Tiny Lights,* and in two previous Silver Boomer anthologies, *Flashlight Memories* and *A Quilt of Holidays.* She is currently working on a memoir. When not writing, she paddles her solo canoe, travels with her husband to out-of-the-way places, visits her nine grandchildren on two coasts, and is a volunteer reading tutor in a Rochester, New York, school.

The Quartet in Waiting
The Editorial Ensemble

soprano and alto keep time
with the beat of submissions
while tenor seems syncopated
and bass waits to the end
then effusing...wrapping
in symphonic harmony
I'd like "haiku" not to be capitalized...
and leave off the title.
What do you mean haiku have no titles!?
Who knew?

There are problems with the "voice"...
is it the house or a cup? What cup?
She says the cups are broken.
I don't buy it. Let's leave it out.

How many ways can we say "waiting?"
...got to have some different titles!
Don't use more than one by that writer...
all her essays sound alike.

This one googles, but
squack is not a real word.
Does it bother the editorially minded?
I hate to mess with the Muse.

Is it the horse or a dog? What dog?
She says the dogs are dead.
I don't buy it. Let's leave it out.

I'm going out of town for the weekend.
I have company coming in.
I'm babysitting grandkids.
I can't get a decent wi-fi signal.

Everybody please weigh in.
155 lbs. Heehee.
No, I mean vote on this...please.
Present.
Sigh

Other Books from Silver Boomer Books

Anthologies

Silver Boomers — *prose and poetry by and about baby boomers*

Freckles to Wrinkles

This Path

From the Porch Swing — *memories of our grandparents*

Flashlight Memories

The Harsh and the Heart — *Celebrating the Military*

On Our Own — *Widowhood for Smarties*

A Quilt of Holidays — *Stories, Poetry, Memoir*

Single Author Books

Song of County Roads
by Ginny Greene

Crazy Lady in the Mirror
by Madelyn Kamen

Books from Eagle Wings Press

imprint of Silver Boomer Books

Slender Steps to Sanity — Twelve-Step Notes of Hope
by OAStepper, Compulsive Overeater

Writing Toward the Light — A Grief Journey
by Laura Flett

A Time for Verse — poetic ponderings on Ecclesiastes
by Barbara B. Rollins

Survived to Love
by Edward L. Hennessy (Ed H)

White Elephants
by Chynna T. Laird

A Cloud of Witnesses — Two Big Books and Us
by Barbara B. Rollins with OAStepper

Insights from the Jobsite
by Robyn Conley

The Innkeeper's Christmas Eve
by Barbara B. Rollins, Illustrated by Sandy Lewis Carter

Books from Laughing Cactus Press
imprint of Silver Boomer Books

Poetry Floats — *New and selected Philosophy-lite*
by Jim Wilson

Bluebonnets, Boots and Buffalo Bones
by Sheryl L. Nelms

not so GRIMM — *gentle fables and cautionary tales*
by Becky Haigler

Three Thousand Doors
by Karen Elaine Greene

Milagros
by Tess Almendárez Lojacono

Haiku Elvis — *A Life in 17 Syllables (or Less)*
by Carlos Colón

Native Voices, Native Lands
by Dixon Hearne

The following selections included in ***Longest Hours – thoughts while waiting***, were previously published, as noted below. The authors retain all copyright to the work.

"Always the Moon," *CC&D Magazine*, August 2009; *See Spot Run*, February 2013 ~ "Ballad of a Coal Miner's Wife," *The Nashwaak Review* 24/25, no. 1 (Summer/Fall 2010): 87-88 ~ "Biopsy," *She Has Something to Say*, Blurb publications, 2008 ~ Jane Blanchard's haiku, *About Place Journal* 1.3, 2012 ~ "Crossings," *Comfort for the Grieving Heart*, 2002; *Chicken Soup for the Caregiver's Soul*, 2004 ~ "Empty Hours," Punclips ~ *"Esperance," Cappers*, 2001 ~ "Even If It Is Godot," poetry chapbook *A Fanciful Geography*, erbacce-press, Liverpool, UK, 2010 ~ "The Floor Moved a Little," previously published as "Waiting" online at *A Small, Good Magazine* January 2012 ~ "Gethsemane," *More God Allows U-Turns*, 2001 ~ "My Leaving Machine is Well-Oiled," *Facing Home and Beyond* ~ "November 22, 1911," *Exit 109*, Old Mountain Press, Sylva NC, 2008 ~ "On Yet Another Birthday," *Chronogram*, and *Creations*, from Ibbetson Street Press, *Facing Home and Beyond, MungBeing*, and *Sarasvati* ~ "The Simple Truth," *The Griffin* (literary journal of Gwynedd-Mercy College), 2011 ~ "Slow Cooking," *Valley Voices* ~ "Storm Front," *2River Review* ~ "That Sound Only," *Soul Fountain*, Queens Village, NY, Volume 40, Fall 2010 ~ "Thawing Ground," *The Chimes* ~ "Through that Door," previously published as "Waiting" in *Boston Literary Magazine*, 2010 ~ "Waiting for a Reply," *Poetry Quarterly*, Spring 2010 ~ "Waiting for the Next Move," August-September 2009 issue of *Alien Skin Magazine* ~ "Waiting Room," *Twisted Dreams*, October 2009; *Flashonomics*, Shade City Press, July 2011 ~ "War, Worry, Wonder, Wait" originally appeared as a chapter in the author's book, *Kaskel Family Memories*, 2011

CPSIA information can be obtained at www.ICGtesting.com
Printed in the USA
LVOW12s2054041013

355462LV00001B/2/P